CONFESSIONS *Of A* CAREGIVER

"Caregivers' Testimonies of Struggle and Perseverance"

COMPILED BY
TWYLIA G. REID

#1 BESTSELLING AUTHOR OF WHAT DO YOU DO…WHEN CAREGIVERS NEED CARE GIVEN.

CONFESSIONS OF A CAREGIVER

Copyright © 2019 by *Twylia G. Reid*. The content in this book is a compilation of the works of the authors mentioned below. The published work is subject to the copyright of each co-author and any attempt to share in part or otherwise any aspect of this book without the expressed permission of all the authors is an infringement of copyright laws. *All rights reserved.*

AUTHORS:
TWLIA G. REID
JILL ARMIJO
TAMARA NEWBORN
ARVINESE REID
TERALEEN CAMPBELL
BARBARA WILLIAMS

Biblical verses are taken from the Good News Translation (GNT), New Living Translation (NLT), and the New International Version (NIV) of The Bible. Quotes listed are from Joyce Meyer of Joyce Meyer Ministries.

Published by WHEN HEAVEN SPEAKS, LLC
Post Office Box 55
Pooler, GA 31322
www.twyliareid.com

CONFESSIONS OF A CAREGIVER / 1st Print Edition
Twylia G. Reid

ISBN: 978-0-578-61101-3
Printed in the United States of America

FIRST PAPERBACK EDITION

Special discounts are available on bulk quantity purchases by book clubs, associations, and special interest groups. For details, email info@twyliareid.com or call (912)335-3799.

DEDICATION

*I dedicate **"CONFESSIONS OF A CAREGIVER"** to the caregivers around the world as a gift of inspiration, encouragement, and motivation to know that we possess the power to indeed move mountains. So, speak life each and every day and watch the changes occur right before your eyes as we continue to grow and travel this journey together!*

TABLE OF CONTENTS

Foreword 3

By Dr. Leif E. Leaf

Introduction 5

Chapter 1 "Lonely Days and Lonely Nights" 9

By: Twylia G. Reid

Chapter 2 "Giving Up the Lies for Love" 17

By: Jill Armijo

Chapter 3 "It's Soo Unfair" 29

By: Tamara B. Newborn

Chapter 4 "Called To Care" 41

By: Arvinese Reid

Chapter 5 "I Didn't Know My Own Strength" 57

By: Teraleen Campbell

Chapter 6 "Keeping It Real" 73

By: Barbara Williams

Chapter 7 "Mirror, Mirror On The Wall" 83

By: Twylia G. Reid

"Caregiver's Affirmation" 97

"Scriptures That Speak Life and Give You Strength" 99

About The Authors 103

ACKNOWLEDGEMENTS

I want to first give thanks and honor to God for gifting me with the anointing, ability, strength, inspiration, desire, and ability to carry out the vision He gave me for this book. You have kept me safe in Your arms, counted my tears, comforted me when no one else was there, and breathed new life into me when I felt like giving up and giving in. For that, I am forever grateful.

Next, I want to thank the amazing women of God who answered the call to share their confessions and testimonies of hope and healing with the world in obedience to God.

To the best friends a caregiver could ever have, you all know who you are…thank you. Thank you for praying for me, for lifting me up, for loving me, for believing in me, for encouraging me, for being a shoulder to cry on, for giving me a safe place to vent, for simply being you. I couldn't travel this journey without you. I love each of you and am grateful to have you in my life.

- Twylia G. Reid

FOREWORD

By Dr. Leif E. Leaf

The role of caregiver is not often seen as something to aspire to. However, the chance to provide others with the love, care, and dignity they deserve can be an opportunity not to be missed. In this book, the many stories and events that caregivers encounter are presented with reality, tenderness, and honesty.

Having known Twylia and Mylon for many years, I have seen the love, patience, and triumphs they have experienced together. In *CONFESSIONS OF A CAREGIVER*, you will find support, encouragement and deepened faith in each story. As followers of Christ, we are told to be encouragers and to shoulder the burdens of those who are suffering. Truly, in *CONFESSIONS OF A CAREGIVER*, it is our hope that you will be encouraged and inspired by examples of faithful followers fulfilling these roles.

CONFESSONS OF A CAREGIVER is a must read!

~ ***Dr. Leif E. Leaf*** is a Psychologist, Clinical Specialist in Leavenworth, Kansas. He graduated with **honors** in 1986 and has more than **33 years** of diverse experiences, especially in **PSYCHOLOGY**.

INTRODUCTION

Wouldn't it be totally awesome to be a caregiver who never gets frustrated and is an unending optimist? I am sure there may be caregivers like that. If you are one of them, I give a standing ovation for your emotional strength and resilience. However, many of us who have provided care for aging or chronically ill loved ones do not fall into that classification. I know I don't.

Each day, we face new challenges and try, once again, to solve those that keep repeating themselves. Caring for a loved one is exasperating and requires a lot of work, and not every caregiver is able to keep a level head at all times. Moments of sadness, frustration, and anger can easily get the best of us and cause our thoughts to take a rather dark turn. Sometimes those thoughts can leave us caught up in guilt wondering, "Did I really just think that?" This can lead you to a place of no return if you are not careful. Simply acknowledging you had the thought and moving on will keep you in a healthy place.

It's important to remember that these negative thoughts are a totally normal reaction to a stressful and sometimes unacknowledged situation. Rather than beating yourself up for how you feel, the key to getting past these thoughts is understanding that you're not the only one who experiences them.

Truly being honest with yourself about how you are feeling both physically and emotionally will allow you to do what's needed to improve your mindset and quality of life. Understandably, some of these thoughts may be more serious than others. You must decide to take charge of your life and not allow these thoughts to control you. Learning how to dismiss and drive out these negative thoughts is vital to your wellbeing.

Experiencing bad or negative thoughts is normal in life, especially in caregiving. You are tired, worn-out, drained, stressed, frazzled, tense, and often being pulled in all directions. However, if you find yourself consistently thinking in this negative manner, it's time for outside help. This outside help can be found in the form of respite care, a doctor visit, perhaps some counseling, and of course plenty of rest and relaxation. Your loved one's wellbeing is important, but remember, you should still be priority number one. If you are not properly taking care of yourself, how can you properly take care of your loved one?

Being a caregiver can be a difficult role. It requires patience, sensitivity, selflessness, and hard work. Providing care for someone, whether it's a child, a parent, a loved one, or as a professional, necessitates a high level of self-love and self-care. Caregiving can feel rewarding and hard at the same time. But while it may be a rewarding experience to care for a loved one, the emotional and physical stress of caregiving far too often leads to burnout and exhaustion, causing caregivers to put themselves and their own well-being in the background.

Caregiving is not a task-oriented role. It is a very active role filled with difficulties and stressors. Caregivers experience dramatic and intense changes in their lives and must acclimate themselves to their new role as a caregiver daily. Why do I say daily? Because, a caregiver's life is forever changing. Caregivers often feel stressed, neglected, and oh yea…very alone. We never know what kind of day we are going to have from the time we get up to the time we go to bed. Therefore, we must learn to be flexible and ready for anything at all times.

Who is a caregiver? Most of us at some point in our lives have been a caregiver. Caregivers are people just like you and I. They are daughters, wives, husbands, sons, grandchildren, nieces, nephews, parents, and friends. While some people obtain care from paid caregivers, most are forced to depend on unpaid care and support from families and friends. Some live in the same house with their loved one, and some live far away. Some may be full-time or part-time. Some caregivers even care for other family members while caring for their disabled loved one as well.

A caregiver's responsibilities can include a number of things, from house cleaning, to cooking and bathing, to managing doctor appointments or finances, to being a best friend, a counselor, and so much more. No matter how much love is between a caregiver and an individual, caregiving isn't an easy job, and it only gets harder as their loved one gets older. Caregiving can take both physical and psychological tolls on anyone, and many caregivers experience symptoms consistent with depression.

Being a caregiver takes a toll on your job, your family's lives, and most of all your personal life. Almost all caregivers at some point may experience anxiety or irritability stemming from their roles, because it is a very demanding job. One of the most important lessons a caregiver can learn is that it is a powerful life-changing enabler for individual growth. What I mean is that once you wear the hat of a caregiver, you will be a different person at the end of it all.

You will look at life through different sets of eyes. You will no longer take for granted the things in life you thought would always be there, like being able to dress yourself or feed yourself. You will learn to appreciate the saying, "This too shall pass." You will understand how perspective plays an important role in your personal growth and well-being. You will learn to deal with the negative thoughts, the dark secrets inside, and most of all you will learn how to thank God for seeing you worthy to wear the crown and hold the title of a *caregiver*.

With that being said, I sincerely wish you all the best as you travel your caregiving journey, and pray that as you read these intimate accounts of caregivers' journeys into the unknown realm of caregiving, their stories of strength and perseverance will empower, educate, and inspire you to keep on keeping on.

CHAPTER 1

LONELY DAYS AND LONELY NIGHTS

By: Twylia G. Reid

*H*e loves me, He loves me not. He loves me, He loves me not. So many days, I have asked myself this question over and over again. *God, why did You allow this to happen?! I know I am not supposed to question You, but why can't I? Why can't I ask You? Well, what I should be saying is, why haven't You answered me. You said I can cast my cares upon You. Soooo…answer me!*

I stopped trying to figure this out years ago. I know God has a reason, He has a reason for everything He does. But damn, why did He have to choose me for this! Yes…I cursed. Every now and then I do because sometimes the frustrations of caregiving take me to a place where all I can do is scream. You'd never understand unless you've walked in my shoes.

The blame game has become a part of my son's and I daily regimen. "It's my fault he can't drive," "it's my fault he doesn't have friends," "it's my fault he's been living with me since he's been born." Those are the ones I hear the most. "It's my fault the accident occurred," "it's my fault he is disabled," "it's my fault he can't work a full time job," "it's my fault he has to take medication," "it's my fault he has seizures," "it's my fault this, it's my fault that! Dang, can I catch a break?"

When this starts to happen it really takes me to a painful place. One I truly try my best to steer clear of. The place where I wonder if I am limiting him from being the best survivor he can be. Am I allowing my fear of losing him again imprisoning him cutting off his ability to live? Am I responsible for things that go wrong? Am I scaring myself about the *"what ifs"* to the point of paralyzing us both from enjoying the *"what is?"*

Guilt is the feeling we have when we do something wrong. Guilt in caring for our loved ones come in many forms. I have probably experienced them all! Guilt over not having done enough to have prevented our car accident in the first place. Guilt over feeling like I want this to end. Guilt over being impatient some days when I had become so overwhelmed to the point of waiting to just crawl under a rock and disappear. Guilt over not loving him unconditionally as I should, or even liking my son at times because he said something to *really* hurt my feelings or because he allowed his frustrations to get the best of him causing him to just have an all-out meltdown. Although this is really common for brain injury survivors, and I know it is, it still made me dislike him for doing it. All this guilt, because I'd become so overwhelmed and just couldn't get myself together! Bad Mommie!!! Yes, I know….lonely days, and lonely nights.

Oh God, not to mention me ever thinking about my own needs. I can't help but see myself as being selfish, especially if it involves going out. Why should I be privileged to go out and enjoy myself when my son can't go out and truly enjoy himself without people judging him because they are too stupid to know about the debilitating challenges traumatic brain injury can cause? Why should I have friends when my son doesn't have any?

Many emotions have surfaced since I took on this job of caregiving.

Frustration is part of many other feelings, such as doubt, uncertainty, anger, and exasperation. Sometimes, as a caregiver, you feel that you can't do anything right or that things just don't go as planned, no matter what you do or how hard you try. This really just makes matters worse. Why, because if you are tired, you are more likely to get frustrated. And, if you are frustrated, you are more likely to adopt unhealthy habits such as stress eating, substance abuse, and a higher likelihood of losing your temper.

The longer you are a caregiver, the more isolated you become. That's just a cold hard fact! I don't care how many books I write, read, or how many counselors I see, this is one truth that will never change. With no one to talk to day in and day out except my son, I felt like I was losing sense of myself. There are a few people I can call on when I'm feeling really low. I normally have to call them because to be honest, I feel they stopped calling or don't call me as much since I often have to say, "Hey, I'll call you right back in the middle of our conversations", or "Hold on a minute let me see what my son is doing because I haven't heard him moving around since we've been talking." Sometimes I just don't call because in my heart I feel they really don't want to hear about it anymore. Heck can you blame them? When I think about it, I guess I really have nothing really to talk about because my life is all about caregiving.

But wait, I'm married! Yea, I am. But…. when put in a situation not of our choosing, it's not uncommon to feel negative and resentful. Little things easily become big things when we feel unappreciated and unacknowledged. While the things necessary for maintaining a strong marriage may be pretty apparent, it is easy for them to fall by the wayside when life gets too hectic and the challenges of caregiving start weighing you down. Neglecting a relationship of any kind, especially marriage, over the long term can result in irreversible and permanent damage.

Any interruption in a longstanding family pattern can be difficult for everyone to adjust to. It may take months or even years to settle into the *new normal* and make changes to get it right. One thing that's for sure is this: patience and understanding are vital for working through these difficult situations together. Just remember to make yourself, your spouse and your loved one a priority while caregiving.

Balance is key. Without it, those lonely days and lonely nights will become your new normal! I am working on this part of my life and since I am confessing…it's one of the hardest things I'm having to do. Having a husband and an adult son to care for is one hell of a job. And, boy oh boy has it taken a toll on me. This journey has caused serious stress on both of us, as well as resentment in us both. Yes, I said it…resentment. In him because of the neglect I know he feels from me. And, in me due to the neglect and lack of understanding I feel from him. But, I must say this, no matter the situation we've weathered many storms and have come out on top, together.

Are the lonely days and lonely nights still there? Absolutely! Have the tears become too many to count? Absolutely! But, knowing that *this too shall pass* is what gives me the inspiration to keep pressing forward. The challenges and hindrances I face as a caregiver are always designed to frustrate and discourage me, but I ultimately decide whether these situations would make or break me. My ability to speak life gets me through many of the toughest times of my life. So, why had I forgotten about this? I do not know. Maybe it was my attitude during those times of testing that affected the outcome of the things I was dealing with.

The day I realized I had more power than I actually understood was June 18, 2001, the day our lives changed forever. Once I understood the challenging situations that accompany my life as a caregiver are *not* designed to make me happy, I was able to move forward in finding ways to make myself happy. The sooner I started thinking positive thoughts, the sooner I was able to move forward.

Yes, I know some of you may think otherwise, but keep in mind, great things happen under pressure and frustration. Many precious, rare, unusual, peculiar, one of a kind, gemstones are formed from rocks being exposed to high temperature and pressure over long periods of time.

So now, I can say that although I still don't quite know why God choose me, I know I love my son unconditionally! Often while riding in the car we sing and dance, laugh, joke, and even argue…a lot! Occasionally he tells me, "I dislike you Mom, but I love you." It's during these times when I know deep in my heart that God didn't make a mistake. At night when he is asleep, I sometimes go in his room and stare at him and thank God for sparing his life. And, ask for God's forgiveness for ever thinking negative or acting ungrateful.

Do I still have lonely days and lonely nights? You bet I do, but I don't worry about them. Instead, I count it all joy when I find myself in challenging situations! Am I crazy? Have I lost it? Of course not! Well, at least I don't think so. I simply realize that most caregivers actually do well under pressure, because it is this fighting spirit that makes the next chapter even better, the next testimony even greater, the next speech more empowering, the next test easier to pass, or the next book…a bestseller. ☺

HOW DOES THIS CONNECT WITH YOU AS A CAREGIVER?

NOW...WHAT IS YOUR CONFESSION AS A CAREGIVER AS IT RELATES TO THIS TOPIC?

_____

_____

_____

_____

_____

_____

_____

_____

_____

_____

_____

_____

_____

_____

"No matter what you're going through there's no pit so deep that God can't reach in and get you out."

— *Joyce Meyer*

CHAPTER 2

GIVING UP THE LIES FOR LOVE

By: Jill Armijo

I was through! Absolutely done with forgiving my husband over and over, finished with listening to him say, "I'm sorry, but …" which in my mind wasn't an apology at all. It was a plea for me to try to see things how he saw them, agree with him, or comply with his plan of action for his current delusion. It meant he was sorry I was upset, not sorry that he was being impossible. And to top off my certainty that his penitence was a farce, he had the nerve to tell me I was stubborn and unreasonable.

I stomped out of the house, pausing this time to put on my shoes and grab my purse and car keys so I could drive around mad instead of walk out in the cold mad, which was my typical modus operandi. I just needed to get away from him following me around trying to convince me that our neighbor was trying to drive us from our home by having friends over who parked in front of our house. It wasn't common that enough friends came over to fill up his driveway and curbside and have to park in front of our house. It happened maybe twice in the four years we lived there.

But my husband, Joe, was adamant.

"We need to call the police," he had said.

"It's not against the law to park in front of the neighbor's house," I told him.

"But I can tell he doesn't like me. He sneered at me when I got the mail yesterday. And he thinks I'm lazy because I use a lawn tractor to mow the grass. He probably wonders why I don't go to work."

"I'm sure he wasn't sneering," I said, "He probably just wanted to talk to you. He's such a nice guy, and he's stuck at home with his leg injury. You two are about the same age, and he could use a friend, so he might have just been trying to make eye contact."

"I can't be friends with him, what are you thinking?"

"*I* know you can't be friends with him, but *he* doesn't know that," I said, exasperated. Joe thought everyone should know how he felt.

"Didn't you tell him about me?" he asked.

"Yes, I told him and his wife about you, but that doesn't mean he knows all of it. I don't even know all of it, and I've been married to you for 15 years! And I live with you. I take care of you. I keep you safe from all the bad guys, and all the good guys that you insist are bad guys.

"So are you going to call the police?"

That was the beginning of the argument that escalated for the next couple of hours. Our three boys each took turns trying to get us to stop arguing. Our youngest covered his ears and closed their bedroom door, trying to tune out our ridiculous tirade. Each time they asked us to stop, I said, "Oh, I'm so sorry, of course we'll stop." I gave my husband the sign of slitting my throat, indicating the argument was over, but he paid no attention to them or to me. He was determined I should call the police.

I tried to make dinner. I took the dog for a short, very cold walk. I asked the boys to come out of their room and tell me about their day.

Each attempt at distraction momentarily provided some peace, but as soon as Joe caught up with me wherever I was in the house, he started in again.

This was *his* MO. Follow Jill around pointing out all the disturbing aspects of Joe's life and brain, and get her to buy into the fear and desperation. It still is his MO, tempered for me now by the fact that he sleeps during most of each day to "stay out of my hair," and watches his conspiracy theory, alien and Big Foot shows at night so he can worry about everyone not paying any attention to all this important information, because it's still a secret.

If I tell him that when it gets on TV it means it's not a secret anymore, he tells me I'm being naïve, and says that just because it's on TV doesn't mean people will believe it and take appropriate action to protect themselves. Right?!

At one point, Joe became angry that I wasn't cooperating and yelled at the kids to stay in their room and quit telling us what to do. Mama bear got angry. I had already been raising my voice and now I was screaming at him to leave me alone. Leave the boys alone, and quit torturing us. But he would NOT quit.

So I left. This behavior had been going on for many years and I was tired. As I drove aimlessly around Covington, Washington I thought, *I can't do this anymore. The boys don't deserve this. I can't get any time alone. I work all day taking care of patients, then come home and take care of him and the kids, and I can't even take care of the kids very well because he needs so much attention. Maybe I should get a divorce. For the boys' sake.* I added that last part to my little tirade of lies to take away some of the guilt I felt at the possibility of leaving him.

It sounded like such a wonderful thing, to be relieved of the burden of caring for him, from having to listen to his incessant fears and irritation about everything anyone said and did. I knew Joe would be on the streets in no time if I didn't take care of him. But as it was, I was on the streets either walking or driving pretty often. It looked to me like it was either him or me on the street, and I preferred it was him. A little voice in my head said it was time to pray. I didn't want to pray. I was angry. I was sick of my life, and I just wanted some peace.

Another little voice said, "You've tried for too long. He's making you miserable. It's time to call it quits."

"Pray."

"Quit."

The voices were relentless. Maybe I was schizophrenic, too. I'd been immersed in my husband's delusions so long; it was rubbing off on me. The truth of the matter seemed to me that I didn't need to pray. It was pretty obvious that it was time to leave him, for my emotional health, and for the kids. I started to cry. Dang it, what was wrong with me?

The problem was I already felt the loss. I'd lost the man I'd married long ago, when he left me on the pier, boarded his ship, the *U.S.S. Acadia* to serve in the Gulf War to liberate Kuwait from Iraq. Operation Desert Storm. He had come back so different, although he hadn't even been in combat. He'd changed from a playful, carefree, generous, and funny guy to a scared rabbit. Oh, he was still funny. He has a great sense of humor as long as he's doing the teasing.

The boys loved their dad. He was the all-time quarterback who took them to Burger King on the way home from the park even though Mom didn't approve. I felt at the moment that all my love for him was gone. Somehow they stole my husband over there in the middle east, and they sent me back a stranger. I wondered if I hated him. It seemed a little strong, but I was really not liking him. I was so tired and so angry! I knew it was time to get out of the relationship. I was living with someone who wasn't the man I'd married.

I parked the car in a parking lot and gazed out at the people hurrying in and out of stores and restaurants in a light rain. It was dark and cold, and before long I had to start the car again to warm up my feet. I let the car run for a while, then turned it off again. I tilted the seat back and tried to sleep. I couldn't. I was fuming way too much. The boys were probably worried, and it wasn't fair to them to stay away so long. I guessed it was time to go home. I didn't want to fight anymore, so I'd wait until morning to tell Joe I was through.

I drove as slowly as I could get away with, which was pretty slow due to the rain and the dearth of street lights on Wax Road. I didn't care about the tailgater shining his brights in my mirror. I felt like I didn't care about anything. Well, except the boys. That's why I was going back home at all. I couldn't leave them. I felt numb. If I could just hold out until they grew up, then they wouldn't be as mad at me for divorcing their dad.

Nope, I was determined. No holding out anymore. Joe's time was up. I pulled into the garage and turned off the car. I opened the door and paused. I was nervous about going in. Would the yelling start up again, or would it just be a bunch of maddening apologies and promises to stop badgering me? With one foot in and one foot out of the car, I sat listening to water drip onto the cement floor. Little droplets drizzled down the windows that the wipers had just barely cleared. The car door dripped water onto my foot.

"Pray."

"NO! I don't want to! I just want to be angry and get a divorce and be left alone."

I grabbed my purse from the passenger seat, got the rest of the way out of the car, and slammed the door shut. Oh crap! I'd forgotten to take the load of laundry out of the dryer. Now. it would be all wrinkled. I opened the dryer, muttering about having to do all the chores, shoveled the clothes into a basket, slammed the dryer door, because that would totally help the clothes get unwrinkled, and shifted the load to one arm as I opened the door to the house.

It was dark and quiet. I turned on a light to find the couch, and dumped the laundry onto it. I'd deal with it tomorrow. I checked on the boys, who were all asleep, two in bunk beds and one in a single bed next to the opposite wall of the master bedroom. Joe and I had agreed that the boys would need the larger space, and we'd taken the smaller room. It was … cozy, with our king-sized bed and dressers, and a tiny closet. I went into our room, where Joe had the nerve to be lightly snoring, sleeping soundly while I had a battle raging in my head.

Now, I decided feeling sorry for myself would be useful. So much for anyone pining away for their missing mother. And Joe seemed to be getting over the trauma just fine. I had to get up for work in the morning and I was late getting to sleep. It was only about 11:00, but I had the habit of getting up early to make breakfast and my lunch, going to the rehab center early to work out and shower before my first patient arrived at 8:00. Nice perk about working at a therapy place, lots of equipment and a warm shower afterward.

I brushed and flossed my teeth, washed my face, and crawled into bed. As I got comfy and snuggled with my pillow, I remembered my prayers. Ugh. I love my Heavenly Father, but I felt small, unworthy, and sick about my tantrum and running off. I'd left the boys to go to bed without homework help, stories, and kisses. I tried to remember whether I had actually gotten dinner all the way ready before taking off. Probably not. Our oldest two were fourteen and twelve, and our youngest was seven. I'm sure they figured something out. We did keep cereal in the house.

"Pray."

Oh, alright already! I carefully climbed out of bed so I wouldn't wake up my husband and knelt beside it. I had a hard time getting started. I felt angry still, and thought I should calm down and try for a little humility and gratitude before addressing the creator of the universe. As I waited to feel like talking respectfully to my Father in Heaven, my knees began to get really sore. It was taking a long time and I was freezing. I climbed back into bed to warm up. I tried to forget about praying, hoping I would just pass out. But I couldn't sleep. I started praying in bed.

I told Heavenly Father that I was sorry I was so angry, but that I felt justified. I told Him I didn't think I was capable of being the wife of someone with mental illness, and that it wasn't good for the boys. I told Him I was going to concentrate really hard on being objective and obedient to whatever it was He told me to do. In a minute, I would get out of bed again and ask a very important question, and it would be nice if I didn't have to wait very long for an answer. It was cold, and I needed to get some sleep.

In retrospect, I'm truly grateful and humbled that with that attitude I ever got answers from God about anything. But I've realized that He doesn't wait for us to be perfect to guide us, and that when we do have to wait for answers it's because we have stuff to learn that helps us fulfill our purpose on Earth and to have more understanding. We wouldn't grow much if every prayer was answered immediately and we were led by the nose throughout life.

As I voiced my question to God, whether I should divorce my husband, I was immediately immersed in a feeling I'd never before felt. It was love, but it wasn't coming from me. It was coming through me, and it was meant for Joe. I knew it was from Jesus Christ, and that it was sent to me to understand how precious and dear my husband is to our Savior.

It was breathtaking. It was incomparable to the love I'd felt for Joe, and that I have our boys, which I had thought was the most powerful love anyone could possibly feel. It was a gift to me. With that exquisite and beautiful manifestation of love beyond description, I realized it was offered to me in my need for respite, to continue in my marriage as though I'd had a year's vacation on a sunny beach. I was restored, and confident, provided with a gift to sustain me and show me my pride and folly in thinking my husband, his illness, or our marriage was a problem. It isn't a problem. It's a means to learn how infinitely loved each of us is in the eyes of God.

With that sensation coursing through my mind, body and spirit, I knew that with God's help, and the evidence of that brilliant light of love, our family could get through all the challenges, because it will be totally worth whatever it takes to experience that love forever.

That experience was many years ago, and I'm sorry to report that I still felt strongly that I should divorce Joe two more times over the years. We're still married, because prayer and the love of Heavenly Father has given me the answers that I've needed both times, which were each very different experiences than that first loving manifestation in Covington, Washington.

Our boys have grown up to become loving, faithful, generous, and kind. They have excelled at their studies, music, athletics, careers, missions, and relationships because of the things they learned from their challenges, not because of a life of ease and comfort. They love and honor their dad, for his sacrifices for our country and for our family.

Joe continues to love me and our boys, our daughter-in-law, granddaughter, and a girlfriend that we hope is soon to be another daughter-in-law. Our youngest is only twenty, but he's just as good as his brothers at choosing loyal and beautiful friends and partners. The future is bright, but will, of course, be riddled with challenges and problems.

Each day is still a journey for Joe and me. We've learned to trade blame for curiosity, judgment for compassion, and feeling stuck for creativity. We've learned that we all want justice – until we need mercy. And we've learned that overwhelm is just our brains' excuse for inaction or too much action.

Our Savior's yoke is truly light and easy to bear, but we have to be willing to share our load and not try to do everything or expect ourselves to be perfect. It's okay to go to bed and leave dishes in the sink. No one is likely to die if I don't vacuum for a month … or two. It's only human to miss a doctor appointment, even if they charge. It's just money. Living paycheck to paycheck and having medical bills pile up until we'll be in debt for the rest of our lives isn't a sin. It's a gift to turn over resentment for forgiveness and peace.

Many miracles with love from God, our family and friends have sustained us. Joe still has delusions. Every. Day. I just love him anyway. I get frustrated and grumpy, feeling like the weight of the world is on my shoulders. And Joe just loves me anyway.

God knows exactly what each of us needs to grow, learn meekness, obedience, and dependence on His perfect plan for us. He knows what will test our faith to the utmost so that we can learn how precious we are – that Christ was not only willing, but powerful enough to suffer and take away our pain so we can repent and partake of His incomparable love, of which I felt a small portion that cold night years ago.

HOW DOES THIS CONNECT WITH YOU AS A CAREGIVER?

NOW...WHAT IS YOUR CONFESSION AS A CAREGIVER AS IT RELATES TO THIS TOPIC?

*"You have to go through
to get through."*

— *Joyce Meyer*

CHAPTER 3

IT'S SOO UNFAIR

By: Tamara B. Newborn

It's soo unfair to be told that the person that you are the closest to, your mother, is diagnosed with cancer and dying within a year and that there is nothing that you can do about it. It's soo unfair that while caring for your mother, you are diagnosed with cancer yourself. It's soo unfair that while continuously caring for your mother and yourself, your sister is diagnosed with cancer and your father is diagnosed with cancer soon after. It's soo unfair that through all of those storms, you have to stay sane and strong enough to make it through the storm because your family depends on it. "No, it's not fair, but everything happens in accordance with God's plan." This is what I had to tell myself over and over again for months as I was hit with storm after storm.

Being a caregiver is very challenging and stressful because you are challenged with balancing caring for someone while taking care of your personal obligations. You are faced with emotions such as anger, depression, and guilt. In most situations, you are so busy caring for everyone else that you neglect to care for yourself. Unfortunately, like most caregivers, I suffered all of the above issues and there were plenty of days that I recited the words, "It's soo unfair." After praying to God and being told that I have to share my testimony in hopes of helping others, I am sharing my story below.

How I Became a Caregiver

For me, it all began in the early part of 2017 when my mother, who had been healthy all of my life, was diagnosed with breast cancer. The lady who had raised 12 kids and assisted in caring for several others was in a position where she needed to be cared for. Being told that she had less than a year to live was a hard pill to swallow. But watching my strong and vibrant mother grow weak and frail was even worse.

My mother was moved to a nursing home in the city that I lived in and, daily, I would sit with her and watch as she lost weight and became a shell of the person I loved more than life itself. This was a hard time for me emotionally, but I knew I couldn't break. My children needed me to be strong while they dealt with losing their grandmother. My children and I would go to work and school during the day and spend the nights at the nursing home with my mother. This meant that we ate dinner and they did their homework nightly there. Our lives had changed.

Several months into caring for my mother, I was diagnosed with breast cancer. Again, I couldn't break because I felt like my family needed me to be strong for them to stay strong. I endured chemo treatments for the cancer that was living within me as I watched my mother go in and out of the hospital due to the effects of the cancer that continued to spread within her. Throughout all of this, I felt like I had to stay strong.

A couple of months into my treatment, my mother slipped into a coma. This happened to be the same day that my sister was diagnosed with cancer. With what little energy I had left, I pushed myself to stay strong because I felt like my family needed me to be. I buried my mother, and within the week, I sat in the hospital's waiting room while my sister had her double mastectomy. I must also add that this happened to be the same day that I had a chemo appointment. Throughout all of that stress, I told myself that I had to stay strong.

Over the next year, my sister and I endured chemo treatments, surgeries, and I had radiation. Following my second surgery, I was told that my father was diagnosed with prostate cancer. No longer could I be the strong person that I had come to be. I cried for a day, which is probably something that I should have done long before now. I eventually picked myself up and did what I had become accustomed to doing and sat in the family waiting room while my father had his prostate surgery.

Challenges I Faced as a Caregiver

It is extremely challenging to be a caregiver. When my mother was first diagnosed, we developed a schedule to care for her. All of us worked and had a family that we also cared for. I was able to hold up my end of the schedule and be there for my mother until I was diagnosed with cancer. Due to all of the effects of my chemo treatments, I was unable to help care for my mother for long periods of time. When I first began my chemo treatments, I was told that I shouldn't be at the hospital because of the risk of infection. I knew that my mother was living in her last days, so I would push myself to get up to go see her.

I faced challenges that I hope no one ever has to face. I did a lot of picking and choosing. There were times where I had to choose whether I was well enough to go visit my mother or not. There were also times where I had to choose whether I had the energy to attend my children's sporting events or not. It was hard for me trying to balance caring for my mother and being there for my children and husband with what little energy I had remaining after my chemo treatments. It was very challenging during those days, because no matter how much I was there for my mother and family, I felt like it wasn't enough.

Guilt I Experienced as a Caregiver

I put a ton of pressure on myself thinking that my family needed me and feeling guilty when I was unable to be there. When I was unable to sit with my mother, I felt guilty. No matter how often I was there with her, I felt it wasn't enough and I worried about her when I wasn't there. I felt guilty that the lady that had taken care of me for the 36 years of my life needed me and I was unable to return the favor. There were also times where I was unable to be there for my children and I felt guilty. It wasn't their fault that I was diagnosed with this ugly disease. I was so tired while going through chemo and I felt guilty because I didn't have the energy for anything else.

I suffered a ton of guilt while caring for my mother, but the hardest part was when it came to deciding the best care for her. It was very important to me that we made the decision that my mother would have made if she was able. The hardest decision to me was deciding whether we should have her removed from the machines or not after she flat-lined and slipped into a coma. Initially, I was ok with her getting assistance from the machines because I thought that there was a chance that she was coming out of the coma. However, when it became obvious that she wasn't, I began to doubt. When my mother was first diagnosed, she told us that she wanted to fight with everything that she had in her, so I wondered if removing her from the machines was taking her right to fight away from her.

My mother was in a coma for over a month before I realized that she was not coming out. Her physical appearance had changed drastically. On top of losing a ton of weight, she had no hair, bedsores, and even though she was in a coma, she lay with her eyes open most of the day. I had no choice but to accept the fact that instead of coming back to us she was transitioning out of this world to be in Heaven with the Lord.

On Thanksgiving of 2017, I experienced the difficulty of celebrating a holiday with a loved one in a hospital. It was hard for me because Thanksgiving was one of my mother's favorite holidays and she spent it in a coma. It was hard for me to celebrate and I dealt with a ton of guilt that day. I felt guilty celebrating anything when my mother was unable and I felt guilty for not wanting to celebrate because it was still a holiday and I didn't want things to change too much for my children. My siblings and I took turns sitting with her that day, but it was not the same as the previous years.

When my mother first left this earth, I felt relief and I felt guilty about that relief. I was relieved for several reasons, but the biggest is that I took comfort in knowing that my mother was at peace in Heaven. I didn't have a meltdown nor did I cry hysterically and I felt guilty because of that.

Consequences I Suffered from Neglecting Myself While Caring for Others

In most situations, the caregiver is so busy caring for everyone else that they neglect to care for themselves. I worried more about what I thought my family needed and neglected to think about myself. For months, I moved off pure adrenaline. Although I was going through storm after storm, I was too afraid to deal with those storms because I was afraid I would break if I did.

The most important thing for me was caring for my mother, and in doing so, I neglected to care for myself. I discovered a lump in my breast a long while before my mother was diagnosed with breast cancer, but instead of her diagnosis pushing me to get the medical care that I needed, I focused on what she needed. I knew if I was diagnosed I wouldn't be able to completely be there for her and that was the most important thing for me.

I was eventually diagnosed with Stage 2B breast cancer and I often wonder if I would have had an earlier stage diagnosis if I would have addressed my issues sooner.

When I was diagnosed and began my chemo treatments, there were days that I would leave my chemo appointments and go straight to see my mother. Even though she was in a coma and didn't know I was there, I felt like she needed me and I definitely needed her. Physically and emotionally, I was a mess. I was going through one of the hardest battles of my life and I didn't have my biggest cheerleader because she was fighting the same battle and losing. When my mother was diagnosed, she refused treatment and I did not; therefore, I felt uncomfortable speaking with her about the side effects of my treatments.

The week of my mother's funeral also happened to be the week that my sister had her double mastectomy surgery. Even though I had a chemo appointment that day and I needed to rest, I couldn't. My sister was going through a storm and she needed our mother, and because she was unable to be there, I felt like I needed to be there in her place. So, instead of getting the rest that I needed after my chemo appointment, I waited around with my family for several hours to see my sister that night.

My sister ended up needing a second surgery. On the day of her surgery, I was emotionally and physically drained, but I had been feeling drained for a few days, so I paid it no mind. With everything going on around me, I couldn't stop. When my sister was wheeled back for her surgery, I went down to the emergency room thinking I was suffering side effects of my last chemo treatment. Unfortunately, that wasn't the case, and within an hour, I was checked in as a patient myself.

The next morning, I was told by the cardiologist that I suffered Broken Heart Syndrome, which is something I'd never heard of before that day. He said that my body was having a reaction to all of the stress and suffering that I had endured over the previous months. When my mother passed, I refused to deal with losing her. My doctor said the grief from losing my mother and the stress of our health issues was the cause of my heart problems.

After conducting research on Broken Heart Syndrome, I learned the following. According to the American Heart Association, even the healthiest person can experience broken heart syndrome. Signs of Broken Heart Syndrome are chest pain and/or shortness of breath. Broken Heart Syndrome may be misdiagnosed as a heart attack because the symptoms and test results are similar. Unlike a heart attack, there's no evidence of blocked heart arteries in Broken Heart Syndrome. Broken Heart Syndrome can be fatal if left untreated.

The week before I was hospitalized, I experienced both intense chest pains and shortness of breath. With everything that was going on at the time, I paid it no mind. I was so busy running from my reality and caring for others that I neglected to care for myself.

Confessions of Being a Caregiver

I confess that on the day that my mother left this earth, I was at peace. Most people won't understand this, but if you have to watch your mother deteriorate the way my mother did, to be in Heaven is the best option. No matter how much I miss her, I know God makes no mistakes.

I confess that even though I know that everything happens for a reason, there were plenty of days while going through the storm that I was sad and angry.

I confess that while I was sitting by my sister's hospital bed a week after burying my mother, I wondered how much longer I could walk through the storm.

I confess that there were plenty of days that I wondered if I would make it through the storm.

I confess that while I waited with my siblings in the waiting room for my father's prostate cancer surgery, two months after I had surgery, I almost wanted to give up.

I confess that I was afraid I would break if I emotionally dealt with all of the storms that were coming my way. So, I didn't!

I confess that there were days while going through storm after storm that I just wanted to give up, and on those days, I said to God over and over, "It's soo unfair."

Life After the Storm

After the passing of my mother, I was stuck wondering what to do next. It was hard getting back to my life before the storm began because I wasn't the same person. I had developed a schedule that I lived by and now that schedule was no longer needed. I did a lot of praying to God for strength and guidance during those days.

Yes, I endured storm after storm, but I decided that I could either let those storms make me or break me. I'm a firm believer that God is in the making business and not the breaking business, so I knew that there was a purpose for my pain. I used the pain that I endured going through the storm to make me the best version of me. On the days when I wanted to cry, I would try smiling instead, and when I was unable to smile, I would cry but pick myself back up and continue to trust in Him and His plan.

I learned that God equips us with the strength necessary to make it through any storm we may face. I believe that our path is predestined by God before we even step foot on this earth. Knowing this, I try to control the things that I can and leave the rest in God's hands.

To whoever needs to hear this, the storm that you are currently facing will end. Just hold on and continue to trust and believe in the Lord.

HOW DOES THIS CONNECT WITH YOU AS A CAREGIVER?

NOW...WHAT IS YOUR CONFESSION AS A CAREGIVER AS IT RELATES TO THIS TOPIC?

"God loves you! He sees what you're going through, He is with you, and He desires to help you right where you are."

— Joyce Meyer

CHAPTER 4

CALLED TO CARE

By: Arvinese Reid

For I know the thoughts that I think toward you, says the Lord, thoughts of peace and not evil, to give you a future and a hope.
Jeremiah 29:11

My Journey as a caregiver started without my knowledge, and you may ask that amazing question, "How could you become a caregiver and not know it?" It was a snowy January morning in a small town in a Hudson Valley, New York, in 1985. I was a high school freshman, when the news was received. A family of four, including a classmate, had been traveling back from New York City was hit head on by another car. This news immediately hit a small town and sent a wave of emotion through a tight knit town. To throw salt to the tragedy, the other driver was the family of another classmate.

Immediately, there was a need for togetherness. The school district supplied grief counseling, but there was another need for togetherness that was necessary for this close-knit town. There were kids that did not want to be alone; some that were even suicidal. That was the moment when another friend and I, with the help of our parents, were able to open our homes to our peers. We provided food and soda, and permission was granted for them to stay as long as consent was given by their parents. We walked in groups to each other's homes and my house was filled with kids that just wanted to be there and deal with what had occurred. We did know how to pray in a group.

The period leading up to the funeral for our beloved friend was filled with long days and nights of another peer and me wiping the tears of our fellow classmates. There were some that even wanted to kill themselves, but the plan of God said not so! We were able to provide a place where we leaned on, counted on, and cried on each other. Believe it or not, a small community made it through a hard and dark time, with peer care. There was a level of care and compassion displayed which was well beyond my experience as a high school freshman. I didn't realize it then, but little did I know that was glimpse into my future. There was a peace I received caring for those people in their time of need. The emotional caregiver can be a draining experience if you totally rely on your own strength. There was a promise from the Lord, that assured us there would be One to come that would be able to carry all our emotional struggles any time we were faced with a situation. I am truly thankful and grateful for that One!

1 Peter 5:7, *"Casting all your cares (all your anxieties, all your worries, and all your concerns, once and for all) on Him, for he cares about you (with deepest affection, and watches over you very carefully)."*

Let's fast forward a few years, college applications, college visits, SAT's, prom, and all the traditions that signaled transition for the high school graduate, or at least for me. I was overly excited and looking forward to my next chapter. I was ecstatic about the idea of living in a dormitory on campus and living my best life. I shared all my dreams with my biggest cheerleader, my mother. She was all in, until I got to the part of visiting a college that was eight hours away. I was angry, and totally unaware she was already experiencing some health issues. Mom did not shut my dorm idea down, but she did say closer colleges would give the same experiences of dorm life. I had my secret resentment, but if you knew my mother the way I did, you knew not to question her. Attending college eight hours away was off the table. I picked a college that was close to home, and definitely was ready to spread my wings!

Graduation was here! The class of 1989 was in full effect! We celebrated and prepared for our "move in" day on campus. You could not tell me anything; I was the apple of Mom and Pop's eyes, and yes I was off to college! I dreamed of the perfect scenario; student by day, and social butterfly on campus events by night. I'd plan to travel home every other weekend with my bestie. We shopped, went to shows, and even enjoyed simple things like sitting and talking. I felt as if my mom was now my "friend," but in the right perspective of course. I shared my academic struggles as well as anything else and I always got sound advice, often in a colorful and amusing sort of way.

In this time period I got my driver's license, Mom even let me drive her around. This was major! My mother did not ride as a passenger for many people, so I was honored she trusted me. Not to long after receiving my driver's license, I noticed Mom was asking me to drive her to doctor's appointments. The first few appointments, I did not go in with her; I sat in the car. The chain of events surrounding these appointments, including the frequency, started to increase. My "visits" home became longer. I wouldn't go back to campus on Sunday because I would have to accompany Mom to her Monday's doctor appointment. Soon after the frequency picked up, I noticed her health was not always good. I asked Mom about her health status and she told me the doctor had informed her she had kidney stones.

Mom's condition did not improve, so she decided to retire from her state job as a food service supervisor. I had to leave school and move back home. My Dad worked overnights and was not comfortable leaving Mom at home alone. I was young, and the thought of leaving college crushed me. One thing that took some of the sting out of the blow of leaving college was thinking that I was being asked to help take care of my mother. They trusted me and felt comfortable that I was able to handle the task. My dad worked at a large pharmaceutical company in our small county. In those days, if your parent was a good employee that meant if their children sought employment they got hired as well. My dad gave me the application to fill out, and a few days later I was hired.

My job was the evening shift; at this point, my mother needed constant care. We worked out with her insurance company and were able to get an aide to come and sit with her for hours in the evening. I had a discussion with my supervisor and advised him that my mother was sick, and I was her *caretaker*. That's when it hit me like a ton of bricks...*I am a caregiver at the age of 20!* Life, as I knew it, was no more; my mother took a turn physically and emotionally that I was not ready for. I would call home in the evenings to check on her, and she would answer the phone crying like a scared child. She would say, "I am doing okay. When are you coming home from work?" Immediately fear would consume me. All I could ask myself was, "Is the aide harming my mother?"

I noticed my mother's behavior declining; she literally became my baby. I found myself very protective of her, and sometimes not wanting to go to work and leave her. There were a few times I asked my boss if could take an extended lunch break and "pop" in on the aide to make sure my mother was not being harmed. Her emotional state was very fragile, I would hear her address my father and brothers saying, "Stop yelling at me." They weren't, by any means, yelling at her, and this was proof things were steady going downhill. I soon became the only one she would respond too. I was watching my strong, weather-any-storm, courageous mother become a defenseless little child who could no longer care for herself. I did not know what to do, but really didn't have time to pity myself much. I threw myself into caregiver mode. my mother could not walk without assistance anymore; she was at a risk of slipping and falling. Her legs became weaker and her fear of falling made walking a huge task for her. That fear soon became a major physical limitation for us both.

I would come home from work and immediately assume my role as caregiver, as my dad was working a lot of overtime to make ends meet. There were times where the aide notified us that all my mom would do is repeatedly ask what time it was. She was literally counting down the time until I got home from work. I was young in chronological age, but I knew that my mother's emotional state needed care.

You see, Mom was not the sit-around type. So, to go from a strong independent woman who held down the house and supported everyone else in the family, driving, cooking, and telling it like it was, whatever that may have been, to being a baby…my baby, was heart wrenching to witness. The way her eyes twinkled each morning melted my heart. We would have breakfast together, and then I would get her dressed, comb her hair, and off we went. That time out would often consist of a doctor's appointment and the grocery store. She would say, "I will sit here and wait for you so I don't hold you up with my slow walking." She absolutely enjoyed being out.

My shift began at 4:00 pm every day. I would go home cook and make sure Mom was settled in before I left for work at 3:15. Honestly, in my mind, I never had the time to think of myself; all I knew was, I had to help Mom. A caregiver at 20 years old, this was not the time to look for a pat on the back, I didn't see it as anything other than normal.

I was always cognizant that the lives my friends lived and even my brothers were very different from mine. My brother's schedule did not change much; he lived with us at the time and did what he could for Mom, but I was the primary caregiver. I can say I did feel alone, often! No one was around who was even close to my age for me to share the biggest highlights of my day with. My mother would cry when I left for work and cry when I came home because she was so excited to see me. This became the highpoint of my day!

My friends were almost finished with college and embarking upon their careers. But hey, it was ok! Besides, I was already working and had a 401k set up as well as my own health insurance. So who needed college? I looked forward to going home to my mother. My friends would comment how strong I was, and they don't know how I did it. Heck, I would think to myself, "I don't know either, but if I don't take care of her who would?" The loneliness I felt, and the isolation became evident. I would lash out at my father and brothers. I would ask them, "What are you so upset about *not* doing? I am the one taking care of Mom!" That's when I knew I needed support. The day-to-day challenges had become too overwhelming.

I advise any caregiver to please not wait until they get to a time where they are lashing out at people before they get support. I had a cousin who would come and hang out with me, sit in the dining room with me and chat while my mom sat in the next room where I could see and hear her. OMG was this *sooooo* needed and appreciated! I would ask my father or brother to sit with Mom on the weekend while I went to the Flea Market with my cousin for a couple of hours. I would come back feeling like a new person, ready to take on my role.

Mom began to go in and out of the hospital. This was into her second year of illness, the episodes of severe fluid retention and periods of not knowing anyone were more frequent. It was during this time I learned to glean more from the Word of God. I would look for scriptures about help, not necessarily for Mom, but for me. In this season, I learned; **Psalm 121:1, 2,** "*I will lift up my eyes to the hills, from whence comes my help? My help comes from the Lord. Who* *made heaven and Earth."*

This role as a caregiver got more intense which required power of attorney documents to be drawn up to handle all of Mom's business affairs. There were times Mom was coherent enough to handle some things on her own, it was those times when important decisions were made. Her doctors knew who I was, and recognized I played an important role regarding my mother's care. This role made me sensitive to the things that were important to her. Also, with the increase in hospital visits, my mother became very adamant about the things she could still control. Things like who fed her, or even who drew her blood. Yes, there were times the hospital would call me, because my mother wouldn't eat until I got there, or refused to have her blood drawn until I got there. The responsibility was great, but we always found a laugh somewhere.

Proverbs 17:22 says, *"A happy heart is good medicine and a joyful mind causes healing, but a broken spirit dries up the bones."* This became my go-to scripture when I needed to remind myself to be joyful through all of this. I spent days and nights and some weekends sitting in my mother's hospital room. It was hard to see that her veins were so small now that the phlebotomists had to resort to giving her needles under her nail and toenail beds. This was the beginning of my agony...hearing her pain, fear, and discomfort expressed in the loudest of cries. There were times when I would just forget about the strong caregiver that I was and cry with her, just not as loud.

One of her last visits to the hospital, my mom was completely out of it. She was talking to who appeared to be an invisible stranger out loud. The doctor said to me, "This is a bad infection, Ms. Reid. Your mother has a high fever, so this can sometimes cause a patient to hallucinate." I heard what the doctor said, but I also knew that this was something else. My mother was saying things like, "I see the light"; "I'm sorry"; and "Yes, I'm ready." I knew in my young mind her communication was not meant for us; she was talking to her

Lord.

Two days later, I got to the hospital and she was out of ICU in a regular room. She talked to me like nothing happened; I was amazed! She said to me, "When you come tomorrow, can you bring my pearl stud earrings, and bring another comb and braid my hair please?" I said, "Of course dear." I thought to myself, *she is feeling good.*

The next day, I walked in the room and my mother's face was radiant. "Wow", was all I could say! I proceeded to put her earrings in and comb, brush, and braid her hair as she asked me to. After I finished, I gave her the mirror she just smiled and put her head back on the pillow and clearly stated, "I'm ready to go home now." I thought to myself, was there a discharge conversation that I missed? I kissed Mom and let her know that I was leaving, and would be back tomorrow.

She said, "Okay sweets, love you." The next morning at 9:59 am, the hospital called me and my family to let us know that my mother had passed away. I exhaled and called the family; I could not help but smile. That was just like my mother wanting to be pretty before she went home. I must say she looked so peaceful and pretty with that same smile of satisfaction she had when I gave her the mirror to see herself after her hair was done, and her earrings were in.

I realized through all of this, the fact I was so young did not negate the fact that the care I gave my mother was from my heart. I did not have a lot of experience and expertise. I can look back with no regrets of missing out on anything. I even realized later that caring for my mother may have kept me from destroying my future in other ways. She left a powerful legacy within her children; I appreciate it as her daughter. I don't mourn her birthday or holidays; I had to change my perspective. I celebrate the traditions she left, holidays are food and fellowship with people that may not have a lot of "natural" family, and make memories.

My father suffered a brief illness, and yet again, here I was in the role of a caregiver. However, this capacity was different. My father had remarried, and his wife was his primary decision maker and caregiver. The role I played as a caregiver was not as hands on as with my mother, but still physically and emotionally supported him, as he was a double amputee with Alzheimer and dementia. His wife decided to place him in a nursing home, as the need for more assistance for my father was great.

The visits were at least four days a week at varying times of the day, to keep the flow of being there. Assisted living facilities stay on their game with patients that have regular visits and have knowledge that at any given time there is someone that will come see this person. Honestly, I had peace knowing that my pops was so near that I could help him, by feeding him his dinner or just sitting and watching his favorite show. I knew that my father enjoyed having the Bible read to him, so I did that as well.

A caregiver's role in any given situation can consist of many things. I like to look at it as being able to give joy to the person in any way whenever you are there with them.

I can say in both parents' cases, I do believe the commandment with Promise that God left for us:

Exodus 20: 12, *"Honor your father and your mother, that your days may be long upon the land which the Lord your God is giving you."* Caregivers of parents have a special call. We don't worry about who is or is not doing their part; we just do what we do with joy from the heart. I assure you God will strengthen you and provide all you need, just trust Him.

Parents are caregivers; the moment that our child is born, we are deemed the role of a caregiver. My journey as a parent caregiver shifted a couple of years ago. My daughter was in college when she developed attacks of migraine headaches. She was a healthy young lady with no known health concerns, other than catching a minor cold every once in a while.

During this particular semester, she was working full time and attending college full time. She lived on campus and commuted to work at the mall. One day, she called me in distress and stated the migraines were unbearable. I asked her to meet me at the closest Urgent Care Center. They suggested she go to the emergency room. The thoughts going through the mind of a 22-year-old, never mind the fact of her mother who is trying not to panic, were all over the place. The migraine she was suffering yielded horrible light sensitivity and excruciating pain for her. I felt helpless and really didn't know what to say or do. I sat in the emergency room with her that night and did what I knew to do in everyday life: I prayed asking the Lord to give her peace and diagnose whatever this was that was causing her so much agony.

A few hours later, the emergency room nurse asked me to step in the hall to clarify information on my daughter's chart. She really asked me to step in the hall to tell me her tests were abnormal and that she needed to be admitted to the hospital immediately. Talking about life jolting, I contacted her father and the journey began. There were different diagnosis and test being run around the clock. These two weeks was taxing and agonizing for my daughter. It was difficult watching her lying there with no energy. Her friends from college came to visit, while her dad and I stayed in shifts between working.

Work served as an outlet for me. I am a Human Service Manager, for Developmentally Disabled Adults, so work helped keep me keep my mind off things as the doctors searched for what possibly could be wrong.

There was one last thing the doctor wanted to test for since her blood count was dangerously low, which was cancer. The leukemia and sickle cell tests both came back negative. Although this was a relief, it was still nerve-racking because the unknown still haunted us. I was able to hold it together emotionally until I saw her on the table for the spinal tap…I was in the hallway with her dad and just broke down crying hysterically. She almost had no blood and we had no answer. I did not doubt the power of Jesus for one minute, and knew He had all power and was able to heal the sick and raise the dead. But, I was still her mother, and an emotional one at that.

The spinal tap was completed, and the doctor who wanted to test for "one last thing" entered the room the next morning. She stated to me my daughter had Paroxysmal Nocturnal Hemoglobinuria (PNH), a rare acquired, life-threatening disease of the blood. It destroys red blood cells at night. And, again just like that, in the blink of an eye this life-changing news placed me yet again in the role of a caregiver! At that moment, I felt I was built for this. What I mean was, I knew right away what needed to be done. As a caregiver, I was thankful that God used the physician to give us the answer. But, I am also a caregiver who knew that even though this condition affects her blood, that I had a relationship with the One (Jesus) who created the blood and gave His life so she can live!

Caregivers, please know that a diagnosis is not your end-all, that person you are caring for depends on you to affirm their goals and help them reach the destiny God has for them.

Hebrews 13:6 says, *"The Lord is my helper; I will not fear. What can man do to me?"* Read, investigate, network, and be informed about the things concerning the person you are caring for. Knowledge is power, and the more you know, the better you can assist them. We read and continue to follow what information is there about her condition, but we have also have witnessed God and His power. My daughter has done some of the things she was told she would never be able to do, which simply astounds the doctors. I am her caregiver, when she doesn't feel well, we help with her twins. I believe God has great plans for her life. Her testimony of hope and healing will also one day help others on their journey.

1 Corinthians 2:9, says, *"But as it is written: Eyes has not seen, nor ear heard, Nor have entered into the heart of man The things which God have prepared for those that love him."*

These experiences I have shared as a caregiver, I believe is part of the plan God has for my life, and each one of them has prepared me for such a time as this. I am Called to Care! Called to speak life into someone that may not understand why Jesus loves us the way He does. **John 10 :10** says, *"The thief does not come except to steal, and to kill, and to destroy, I come that they may have life, and that they may have it more abundantly."*

My confession: I experienced several emotions that almost caused me to quit: hopelessness, helplessness, isolation, anger, betrayal, and even rage. There were times I wanted to give up and give in, but I didn't. There were days I wondered why life for me was the way it was at such a young age. You will get tired, weary, and even frustrated. These are real feelings. There were times I cried out to God asking Him, "Weren't my parents enough, why my daughter, too!" Although the feelings may become overwhelming, don't quit, seek help. Jesus will give you the peace, joy, and the sound mind that you deserve and crave. You must learn to rely on God, in spite of the challenges you face. Keep your eyes on Him!

I leave with you, the scripture that I opened this chapter with, there is no other way for me to say it, you are not alone! You are thought of and loved by the Man who is above every man, Jesus!

Jeremiah 29:11 tells us, *"For I know the thoughts that I think toward you, says the Lord, thoughts of peace and not of evil, to give you a future and a hope."*

HOW DOES THIS CONNECT WITH YOU AS A CAREGIVER?

NOW...WHAT IS YOUR CONFESSION AS A CAREGIVER AS IT RELATES TO THIS TOPIC?

"Courage is fear that has said its prayers and decided to go forward anyway."

— Joyce Meyer

CHAPTER 5

I DIDN'T KNOW MY OWN STRENGTH

By: Teraleen Campbell

Wishful thinking!

I truly wish there was more knowledge and awareness in our society about caregiving. I say this not seeking pity, rather because awareness is sorely needed. Many people are caregivers; however, they don't know it. Many believe that their relative or loved one must reside in the same home in order to be a caregiver. However, leading caregiving organizations now define caregivers as those who provide either specific or broad care for someone else. This care may include: physical, legal, or financial areas.

Acknowledging that a change has occurred in lifestyle is a major, first step. Recognizing the shift in one's life then reassessing priorities and making necessary adjustments is critical. It helps alleviate higher levels of burnout and resentment.

In my case, I had to reprioritize my finances. We also had to liquidate what little assets my mom had because she needed the long-term care that Medicaid would have to cover. Once it had been approved, her monthly disability allotment went directly to the nursing facility, leaving only $72 for other needs. This meant I had to step in and cover her clothing, cell phone bill (otherwise we had no method for direct communication), personal care items, and life insurance, for example.

People often have very little understanding of how taking on a caregiving role impacts our lives. For example, there are the days missed from work sometimes without pay. Some do not understand when caregiving obligations require adjustments to social schedules, saying NO to invitations, and not being able to hang out.

I wish people understood that caregivers' disposable incomes may take a hit. They may simply be too tired to attend some events. Initially, I pushed myself to the limit, which led to me almost falling asleep while driving on numerous occasions. As time went on, I became grateful for friends who made the drive to visit my mother with me. People must remember that the priorities of caregivers have shifted. The person for whom they are caring becomes their highest priority.

I also wish employers made provisions in leave policies for caregivers. While I may not have been sick, I was caring for someone who was. That required a great deal of my attention. As a caregiver, I had to keep my phone nearby, as the doctor or nursing facility could call at any time. I honestly contemplated taking FMLA, not because of too many work absences, rather because the struggle not to miss work began to overwhelm me.

How did I get here?

In most cases, ascending into the role of caregiver comes suddenly. My mother went to the hospital for a routine hernia repair surgery. She came through the procedure fine. I visited her in the hospital and she was doing well. When I called the next day to check on her, an ICU nurse picked up the phone. I thought I had been transferred to the wrong unit because Mom was not in ICU when I left her. This had to be a mistake; however, it was not. The nurse informed me my mother had developed an infection called Sepsis which was causing her vital organs to shut down. She had been placed on life support, where she remained for more than two months. She also required dialysis for one month due to the fact that the infection affected her kidneys. She'd never had kidney problems! All of this was unreal to me. My mom was semi-conscious at one point and made it clear to me and my cousins that she was *not* ready to die. That was all that I needed to know to hang in there with her and fight.

We prayed for God not to let her die. He answered that prayer. My mother endured 6 abdominal surgeries. She had part of her colon removed and received a colostomy bag. The bag was later removed after she improved. Doctors told me she would have no quality of life. We posted healing scriptures in her hospital room, spoke the word over her, and prayed for God to touch her body, and He did! Doctors said she would never walk again, but she proved them wrong and did! Although she survived, my mother required the type of medical attention that could be provided by a nursing home. Alas, she spent the last 6 years of her life in a nursing home and our lives were never the same. This began my ascension to the role of a caregiver.

There often is no warning or time to prepare. I am sure that I speak for 99 percent of caregivers when I say I wish we could have been more prepared. However, the reality is that no one really forestalls it happening to them. Most people do not expect a day when they are alive, yet unable to care for themselves. At the same time, most of us do not anticipate becoming a caregiver.

After the prayer is answered, what next? I can honestly state that I wasn't ready. When a loved one becomes ill, we typically call forth our prayer warriors. We ask God to heal them. While, of course, healing is the ultimate goal, we don't consider the ramifications and side effects (if you will) that accompany the healing. In essence, the devastating changes to the lives of both individuals need to be considered along with the impact on the lives of everyone. This impact could include areas of their health, sleep, finances, and social life in addition to other facets of one's lifestyle.

My mother endured a great deal of trails during her life. She overcame domestic violence, divorce, serving as primary caregiver for my grandmother, then subsequently dealing with her death. She also lost three of her closest friends who were more like sisters. I remember how the last friend passed away after being unable to locate a bone marrow donor. Due to my mom's professional medical background, she helped take care of them all during their final months. The tears, the grief, both of us were extremely sad after they passed away.

Not only was my mom a strong woman, but she was also a great woman of prayer. I gleaned my strength from her. However, it nearly crippled me when her health took a major decline nine years ago. Ironically, I continued a fairly hectic pace in my own life, while taking on this new role of caregiver. Therefore, most people did not realize that I, myself, was struggling! Although God was elevating me in ministry, I was truly struggling with my new life's reality.

Cindy (my mother) was the strongest woman I knew. She had fought to get her life back after her ex-husband literally tried to take it. She had overcome so much! Seeing her become dependent on me and a medical staff weakened me. I was not ready, at least I didn't feel ready. Psalm 46:1, *"God is our refuge and strength, a very present help in trouble"* became my daily declaration.

Once I got over the shock and awe of the situation, I realized that I could not buckle because she needed me! Imagine that, the person who birthed and raised you now needing you! I thought to myself, "This is not a dream. This is real life, just wow!" I followed my mommy's example and prayed. Gradually, I began to feel the Lord renew my strength. I recall thinking, "So we are really here, Lord. Okay, let's do this!" To be perfectly honest, I wasn't really certain what "*this*" meant.

Nurses wanted me to consider taking my mother off life support. Being the only child, I had no siblings to consult. I felt incredibly alone, although I had friends and other family who were very supportive. At the end of the day, the responsibility fell on me. I prayed and asked God to help me make the best decisions.

As my mom made gradual progress, another set of decisions needed to be made. With each decision came a new set of challenges that seemed to deplete my strength. I can now say that every time it felt as if I had nothing left to give, strength and a greater resolve to care for my mom came from somewhere! I know it was God!

There are dynamics to caregiving that are rarely discussed. Here are a few:

- The family - Caregiving takes a toll on families. The truth of the matter is, some family members are not up to the challenge of being a caregiver. I will say up front that coming to this realization was a hard pill for me to swallow. I simply could not imagine being inactive when it came to ensuring the well-being and care of someone for whom I professed to love. There was no way that I would defer my mother's care to someone else.

  Over time, I have come to realize that some truly do love the other individual. However, they may not have the capacity to do what we do and have done. Although I would like for things to be different, that is not the case. I would much rather have people bow out than to be abusive to the ones for whom they are caring. Sadly, I have read too many stories regarding abuse of the elderly and those who are disabled. Many times, that abuse is at the hands of caregivers who are burned out or should have never been given the responsibility in the first place.

My prayer for anyone who is living in the reality of being a caregiver while others have opted out is that the spirits of anger nor bitterness overtake you. I encourage you to roll with what you know is *right*! Rest assured, the effort you put forth will not go unnoticed or unrewarded.

- The personal impact - Being a caregiver is exhausting and lonely. People often think that a break in a caregiver's schedule frees them up to hang out and socialize. While this would be nice, this is not always the case. One of the best things about having free time is the opportunity to rest!

    There have been times when I was sooooo tired that I could not think straight. It is one thing to be tired, but another to be exhausted. Sometimes the exhaustion transcends physical to emotional and mental.

- The turmoil – I became too engrossed in caring for my mother that I realized I had lost part of myself. A large part of my life became absorbed in supporting her. After coming to this realization, I felt conflicted as to how and if I should go about rediscovering Teraleen. I felt torn. Trying to balance my life, my needs, working toward my goals while fulfilling my responsibilities was overwhelming and very challenging. Self-sacrifice was primary, while self-care became non-existent.

- The harsh reality – The day that a caregiver stops sacrificing themselves will likely be the day that their loved one departs their Earthly life. Yes, I did think about this – often. As the years went on and with each Christmas, Thanksgiving, and birthday, I was not only grateful. I was secretly fearful. I privately asked God how much more time I had with my mom. I did my best to ensure that she felt loved and appreciated during those last 5 Christmases and birthdays. Part of my motivation was the private thought that it could be the last one. I never told anyone what was going through my mind. I was living in a secluded emotional purgatory.

I even rehearsed in my mind whether it was best to be with her whenever she made her transition or how it would feel to get that dreadful call from either the hospital or nursing home. In the end, I was, along with other family members, present during her final weekend. Signing hospice papers was like an out-of-body experience for me. Once reality set in, we made her room as peaceful as possible, singing hymns and playing the gospel songs that she loved so much until she made her transition. Afterwards, I let out a scream that was unmatched. I wailed! It was over. My time as a caregiver had ended.

At the end of the day, I needed to have the peace of knowing that I had done my absolute best in terms of caring for her. She had given me so much and instilled so much in me. No matter how challenging, I felt as though this was my reasonable service.

Tips from Teraleen

1. Although overwhelming and at times stressful, I encourage caregivers to be as involved in the care of loved ones as possible. Although I could not attend every one, I attended as many care plan meetings at her nursing facility as possible. I actually lived and hour and a half away from my mother; therefore, I made arrangements to hold most of the meetings via conference calls since they were held on weekdays.

2. Should you have aging parents, encourage them to get their affairs in order. Additionally, make sure that yours are in order. Through it all, one level of pressure was alleviated from me because my mother had an active life insurance policy. Not only that, but she told me where to find the insurance paperwork. Be sure to get durable power of attorney documents. This will enable you to handle business on their behalf should your loved one be unable to do so.

3. If your loved one is in a facility, do not be afraid to advocate on their behalf. Get to know the charge nurse, administrator and ombudsman.

4. Change up your schedule. Do not limit visits to evenings and weekends. I periodically took off work and visited my mother during the day – unannounced. I chuckled when I saw the looks on staff members' faces.

5. Accept assistance when offered. Being the daughter of an independent woman, I too am just that. Coupled with being an only child, I had grown used to doing things myself. There were times when I was simply too exhausted to make that three-hour round-trip drive to see my mother, but knew it was necessary. I learned to ask for and accept support from a sorority sister driving me or someone sending me a gift card to help with gas money. Instead of my previous "I'm alright," I learned to accept the support and say "thank you."

6. Schedule time for yourself. The concept of self-care became important to me after I attended an AARP workshop. During that session, I learned that a significant number of caregiver either become seriously ill or die while serving as caregivers. I, along with most in the room were startled. It became painfully clear that I was all she had. If something happened to me, then she would be put into a worse situation.

Confessions of this Caregiver!

Confession: Caregivers often feel inadequate

There were times when despite the "*at a girl*" and accolades, I felt totally inadequate while caring for my mother. I second-guessed myself. I wondered whether I was doing a good job. I wondered whether I was present enough. One of my goals was for my mom to maintain as high level quality of life as possible. I wanted her to maintain some level of independence, but doing so caused me to question myself.

The feelings of inadequacy led to me feeling distant. I retreated and went into a cocoon, oftentimes not physically, but certainly emotionally. Most around me did not notice. I am grateful for my core group who know how to give each other space, but will pick up the phone if we have not spoken in three days.

Profession: God is more than enough when I am not enough. As servants, first of God, then as we serve our loved ones, we are overcomers, even conquerors.

2 Corinthians 12:9, Each time he said, "My grace is all you need. My power works best in weakness." So now I am glad to boast about my weaknesses, so that the power of Christ can work through me.

Confession – becoming a caregiver impacts the way that others relate to you.

Perhaps it's the fact that people don't know what to say. Perhaps they don't understand the magnitude of what you are dealing with. Perhaps they don't care. Perhaps it is a combination of the three. I know there were times when people asked me to assist them with something or attend an event and I had to say no. Unfortunately, my nos were not always received with understanding or empathy.

Profession: I appreciate the fact that God understands especially when it seems like others don't. I maintain confidence in God and am at peace.

Isaiah 32:17, "And the work of righteousness shall be peace; and the effect of righteousness, quietness and confidence forever."

Confession: Caregivers sometimes feel like they are a failure:

Profession: I speak courage, success, and strength to myself. God is helping me right now. I cancel feelings of defeat. I get closer to God. I stand on *James 4:7-8, "Resist the devil and he will flee from you. Draw nigh to God and He will draw nigh to you."*

I also stand on Psalm 42:11, "Why am I discouraged?" Why is my heart so sad? I will put my hope in God! I will praise Him again - my Savior and my God!

Confession: Caregivers wrestle with a variety of emotions including anger and anxiety.

Profession: The peace of God helps maintain mental health and stability. I stand on Isaiah 26:3, *"Thou wilt keep him in perfect peace, whose mind is stayed on thee: because he trusteth in thee.*

Confession: Caregivers sometimes feel deserted.

Profession: Although I may be alone now, I am not deserted or forsaken. I stand on *Hebrews 6:10 and 2 Corinthians 4:8-9, "For God is not unjust. He will not forget how hard you have worked for him and how you have shown your love to him by caring for other believers, as you still do."*

We are hard-pressed on every side, but not crushed; perplexed, but not in despair; persecuted, but not abandoned; struck down, but not destroyed.

Confession: Sometimes there is too much information, yet not enough provided when it comes to considering best courses of care for our loved ones.

Profession: God will crown my head with wisdom. *"For the Lord grants wisdom! From his mouth come knowledge and understanding. He grants a treasure of common sense to the honest. He is a shield to those who walk with integrity. He guards the paths of the just and protects those who are faithful to him." Proverbs 2:6-8*

Confession: The circumstances under which caregivers live can overshadow our faith in God and cause us to lose hope.

Profession: Although some days are very difficult, I will not let my situation overshadow my faith in God. I stand on *Mark 9:23-24, "What do you mean, 'If I can'?" Jesus asked. "Anything is possible if a person believes. "The father instantly cried out, "I do believe, but help me overcome my unbelief!"*

Confession: Caregivers worry about the end.

Profession: No matter how it turns out, as long as God is with me things will work out for me. I stand on *Romans 8:28, "And we know that God causes everything to work together for the good of those who love God and are called according to his purpose for them."*

Conclusion

I reflect on a day when I was sitting in my office and Whitney Houston's last CD was playing. A song began to play and Whitney kept repeating the works, *"I didn't know my own strength."* Whitney went on to proclaim in the song, *"I was not built to break."* Whew Lord! That song almost had me on the floor. Tears streamed down my face. It was as if the song had become my testimony.

I remembered whose daughter I was. I recalled how much adversity I had seen my mother overcome. I thought of the things she had instilled in me. I told myself that I was not built to break!

Yes, caregiving is challenging. We may end up with more problems and questions than answers and solutions, but rest assured that just in a nick of time, God will give you the strength to make it through! I am a living witness!! God will grace you to move in a manner that surprises and makes you proclaim, "I didn't know my own strength!"

One thing that I realized during this journey is even on the days when I felt weakest, God would send me strength from somewhere that enabled me to carry out my responsibilities. For that, I am so grateful!

Every time I think about those days, the words of Whitney's song reverberate in my spirit. *"I didn't know my own strength."* It was revealed to me that it really was not my own strength. It was the strength of the Lord. In other words, the Lord gave me a fresh dose or boost of strength! I was able to serve, not so much from my own strength, but it was the strength that God imparted to me. I recognize that He was pouring strength into me when I wasn't aware. I did not recognize the fresh dose until I actually needed it.

Likewise, caregiver, God will embolden you to care for your loved one. He is pouring into you even now. On those days when you feel as though all strength has been depleted and you want to sleep the day away, but know you cannot, God will make that stored-up dose of strength available to you. You will get through those days, then look back and say to yourself, *"I didn't know my own strength."*

#celebratingcindymo

HOW DOES THIS CONNECT WITH YOU AS A CAREGIVER?

NOW...WHAT IS YOUR CONFESSION AS A CAREGIVER AS IT RELATES TO THIS TOPIC?

"If you will do the little bit you can do, God will do everything that you cannot do."

— Joyce Meyer

CHAPTER 6

KEEPING IT REAL

By: Barbara Williams

"Then you will know the truth, and the truth will set you free" John 8:32 (NIV).

As the R & B singer, Usher Raymond says, "These are my confessions!" Yes, facing my feelings during my journey as a caregiver for my mom is my new normal, so they say. But to me this is not my normal. Who would have thought that in January 2017 my life would change so dramatically? Who would have thought that my rock, my heart, my ride or die, my BFF, my mother, would get to the point where she no longer knew me, her only child on a consistent basis?

Mom's mental state began to decline slowly with the misspelling of words, not able to say words that she wanted to say and I watched with frustration. I saw how frustrated she got when she couldn't say certain things and would say, "You know what I mean." When she would forget how to fill in her checks, write out her bills correctly, not be able to order a meal at a restaurant...this broke my heart. "Where are we going?" "Have I been here before?" are questions she often asked while we were out. When shopping at our favorite mall, she would say, "This is nice, how did you know about this place?" Every time we went out, my heart would break over and over again because it was like this was a new adventure for her. Mom was my driver shuffling me everywhere, so for her not to remember her usual routes was completely devastating to me and I can only imagine what was going on in her head.

Anyone who knew my mom knew that she was a jazzy, outgoing, outspoken, funny First Lady who loved shopping and helping others. *Ms. Anne*, as she was called, taught me to be who I am today. I learned how to be the wife and mother I am from the examples she set. She always encouraged me to be the best that I could be.

The strongest example I witnessed of her strength was one Sunday, May 15th, 1977, after my father, the late Rev. Ovis Flournoy, gave his text and spoke about the love he had for my mom and then passed away in the pulpit during the sermon. From that day on, it has been my mom and I. Many said I would go astray after my daddy died, but Mom was no joke!

She worked hard to push me through high school since I was a freshman when my dad passed. She supported me through college working as a nanny and housekeeper to ensure my tuition and supplies were paid. I have always been proud of her especially when she was in her 70s because she was the oldest student in her class, *and* scored the highest score to become a licensed Home Health Aide, a job she worked well into her 80s!

I never imagined that dementia would destroy the mom I always knew. My outlook on my retirement was, *Now, we can travel the world!* This was an adventure I had hoped Mom and I would go on. Due to the sacrifices she made for me, I knew I needed to retire in order to be able to take care of her since I was in a position to do so, and had the blessings of my husband, Noble. But it has not been without some emotional struggles, depression, and questions! "Lord, why my mom?" "I don't think this is fair to my mom, my family or me!" "WHY...LORD...WHY?"

As I watch her decline on a daily basis, so many emotions and questions rush through my mind. The emotions I have experienced through this journey keeps me on a rollercoaster. I was now a caregiver, something I could have never imagined but I'm glad to experience this because I am learning a lot about myself, my mom and my Faith Walk has increased.

I have personally experienced frustration, pain, hurt, disappoint, and challenges that not only came from friends, and family...but church members. I have always heard it said, "There is nothing like, church hurt," but I thank God for my Divinity Missionary Baptist Church in East Orange, NJ and our leaders Pastor, Dr. Byron E. Lennon and First Lady, Dr. Margaret Lennon, because this is the place where my healing has taken place.

Never would I have ever imagined that I would be so overwhelmed at times. Lack of sleep, lack of understanding as to why I can't participate in this or that. Lack of people just letting me vent without making me feel guilty. "Why, Lord?" Yes, I try to put up a good front, but deep down, I'm hurt, I find myself crying and at times I'm even angry. "Lord, why Me?" "Lord, how can I minister to your people when I don't feel like it?" On Sundays when the choir sings, and I hear the introduction to the song I lead being played, the question pops in my mind: "How can I sing, **'The Storm is Almost Gone,'** when I'm sitting in the midst of my storm?" And, "Please don't let anyone ask me to pray today"! "Lord, am I sane, can I really handle this?" "Lord, how long?" Is it so bad that I have these questions and how I react at times? Yes, my actions at times have caused me to question myself.

And because of my rollercoaster emotions, I might be a little short-tempered and take things out on my husband, kids, and others when I don't intend too. I find myself sometime overapologizing when I really want to scream: **"Can't you see what I'm going through and can't you be a little more understanding!"** **"Just let me be!"** Then the tears begin to flow because I realize I just want my mommy! Not like she is now, but I have prayed to have one more meaningful conversation with her. I miss her, the real her, and not the shell of the person that lies in her bed and stares at me each time I enter into her room. I miss her cooking big meals and asking me if I had a great day! I miss her pop up surprises to my classroom, and engaging in conversation with my students and coworkers! So I lock myself in the bathroom or hide under my covers with a tear stained face and broken heart because this little girl wants her mommy!

It's during these times, Noble, my husband, helps to restore my sanity and makes sure we go out at least once a month. Thank God! My daughters make plans to stay with their Nana and sends me out with my sister/friend, Maggie Baker so I can regroup. They all try to help me regain and enjoy myself. Maggie lets me vent, cry, get angry, but then comforts and prays with me, and helps me laugh.

Yes, my confessions! No sympathy needed it's just time people understand that being a Christian, wife, mother, grandmother, aunt, sister, minister and a caregiver is not easy. We have emotions and feelings like everyone else! We suffer, we hurt, we cry and we struggle with what we experience and face in our lives. Pastor Byron Lennon said: "Don't let them tell your story! Tell it yourself because they might get it twisted!" It bothers me when people feel that as a Christian you should not question God…but hey, I am still human! My confession!

The hurt is really overwhelming. People that you thought you could count on are long gone and have disappeared. When my mom first started experiencing dementia, the calls were coming on a regular to check up on her, but then nothing. "What happened to everyone?" I'd often think. I can count on her brother, sister-in-law, and sister checking on her on a regular basis, but they are up in age and are dealing with their own health issues. There are also nieces and nephews who are out of state that check on her. And, I really appreciate those calls! Heck, I actually need them.

This was the greatest hurt I felt. Yes….abandonment is what I see it has. But I'm happy to say, after reading *When Caregivers Need Care Given* by Twylia G. Reid, and listening to my pastor, Dr. Byron Lennon's sermon, I'm finally at peace with it! This incident had me hurt, which turned into anger, which turned into resentment…But God!

My mom being a former First Lady remained at the church which my father organized after his passing in 1977. I expected so much from this congregation because they were always so loving, kind, one big happy family. She attended until she could not physically go anymore to the decline of her mental status. Mom loved that church and the people there and always wanted to attend. When I tried to talk to her about attending church with our family, she did not want to hear it. She had so many memories. One faithful member would pick her up and bring her home, since my husband and I were a part of another ministry or my daughter would drop her off and pick her up. As her memory declined, no one else offered to transport. One thing I learned quickly is that when you are older and can no longer attend regularly, you are forgotten.

Being from the *old school*, I was used to my father, deacons, and deaconess of the church visiting the sick and shut in and bringing communion to them. I just figured this would continue, but when this was not done I was so hurt….and even a bit salty! My mind kept replaying all the times my mom visited and called the members who could not make service, and I just expected the same to be done for her. I found my hurt turning into anger and then resentment. "Lord, what's wrong with people?" "Why haven't anyone called or checked on her?" Receiving a text asking "how is mom and can we visit or call" was great but the visit never happened and a year passed and another text "can we come see her one Sunday?" Now it's almost another year and *that* Sunday visit *still* hasn't taken place.

I have learned to not put my trust in any man. This incident really did something to me, but God had to really do a work on me! I was hurting for her! But this pain and hurt was so real, and I didn't know what to do with it! At one point, I just wanted to tell everyone associated a piece of my mind. But, God did a mighty work in me and with me! I have totally surrendered this hurt to God and He has truly delivered me and healed my hurt and anger with this situation.

I was holding on to the messages and every time I looked at it I got angrier and angrier. Although it was difficult, my first step was deleting them. I let go and prayed for those who I felt caused this hurt. I realized I can't be angry with you because I'm praying for you. This changed my heart towards this situation and people. I realized that I also had to ask for forgiveness and pray for myself. I had to literally detox my heart, and this freed me!

My confession! It was a process and didn't happen overnight! I didn't just say, "Lord forgive them," and 1, 2, 3 things were better. This took a while, but I have made it through this hurdle. All of the hurt, pain, and disappointments have not gone away, but I'm learning day by day to let go and let God.

"Was I wrong?" God really had to show me how to handle this because I felt this to the core of my heart. One thing that I'm finding out is no matter how many questions I may have, I am never alone. God assures me that He will never leave me nor forsake me. In one of his sermons, Dr. Lennon said, "God does not put you through anything and leave you, but He equips you for whatever ministry He places you in." So, I went to God and asked, "Lord, are You saying that my caregiving in not my new normal, but my ministry for this season?" And, He quietly answered, "Yes, my child!"

With this new outlook, I can now boldly declare, "My caregiving journey is indeed my *ministry*, and not my new normal!" God is steadily equipping my for such a time as this. I am in a church where there are families that have loved ones with dementia, and the outpouring of support I receive is amazing. But, I still have questions at times. Even as I write my confessions, my mom has been in the hospital and has just been released under hospice care. I have gone to God and asked, "Lord, am I able to let her go?" "Lord is she suffering"? "Why, Lord, Why?" "Lord, can I handle this and be strong for my children and grandchildren?"

After much prayer, reading the Word of God, and communing with Him daily, I feel His loving arms around me. Lying in the bed with Mom and listening to gospel music, there is peace that is surpassing all understanding. I listen to His voice and I can truly say that I have been filled with so much peace and comfort. He will keep him in perfect peace whose mind is stayed on Him. I am a living witness that He will give you peace that surpass all understanding.

I want to encourage you who are reading this. Questions will come and your emotions may be a rollercoaster, but God is in control. Don't think that those in ministry who are caregivers are not going through bad situations like you. I want you to know we are human, we experience hurt, pain, anger and depression. We have questions that we want answers to. Remember to trust God with your situation. My confessions!

HOW DOES THIS CONNECT WITH YOU AS A CAREGIVER?

NOW...WHAT IS YOUR CONFESSION AS A CAREGIVER AS IT RELATES TO THIS TOPIC?

"Our worst day with God is still better than our best day without Him."

— *Joyce Meyer*

CHAPTER 7

MIRROR, MIRROR ON THE WALL

By: Twylia G. Reid

I am constantly shifting my focus from one thing to the next. Whether it's person to person or task to task, I truly never know if I am coming or going, or going or coming! I am constantly trying to balance caregiving, being a wife, being a mom, being a Nana to our grandchildren, being a loving caring daughter and big sister, my career, my ministry, errands, housework, our dog Zyn, school work, ugh....it all!!! I never have time for myself. Not even time to catch a breath let alone do something I really enjoy doing.

I am 52, and retired from the military after serving 20 years! How many people can say they are retired at the age of 52? Yes, several I know…but how many can say it but choose not to disclose because it doesn't feel like it nor are they able to truly experience the enjoyment of it? When I was little, I used to dream of what life would be like when I got old enough to enjoy the fruits of my labor. I was a teenaged single mother who started working at the age of 15. I had my daughter when I was 17 years old, and my son when I turned 21. So all the things I could not do for them due to the lack of experience and knowledge of raising a child I vowed to do when I became older.

As a child, I used to see couples on TV boating, traveling, simply enjoying life. I always told myself that one day I would do the exact same thing and not have a care in the world. You know, things youngsters fantasize about but really don't have a clue as to what it really takes to obtain a carefree lifestyle like that. I remember when I first joined the military, I dreamed of all the places I would travel after I did my time and retired. I dreamed of the life I would give my children and grandchildren. All the things my parents were not able to do for my siblings and I, I had planned to do for my own children. Nothing elaborate, you know things like making sure they had the opportunity to experience the world and various cultures. Making sure I spent quality time with them teaching them about the world and the things of the world. Taking family trips was something I always said we would do. I never wanted them to feel confined or limited to the environment surrounding them. I wanted them to have the opportunity to explore the world and all it had to offer. My parents were great providers and did all they could to ensure my siblings and I had what we needed, but traveling was something we never really got to do. It wasn't until I joined the military that I took my first airplane ride. So, I had BIG plans for my family.

Unfortunately, our accident occurred long before I even made it to the half way mark of my military career. When I tell you it changed my life and every aspect of it…please believe me it did! My military career came to a screeching halt. Although I was able to stay in and serve my country, I was limited to the schools, courses, and programs available to me that would aid in the advancement of my career. This forced me to sit back and watch my peers excel well above me. Soldiers who were once underneath me, whom I was responsible for training and development, who looked to me for guidance and direction, were now above me. I was now answering to them. How embarrassing was that! Having to be moved from office to office because of this was too much to bear at times. The shame would often cause me to pretend to have appointments when I didn't just to avoid being in the presence of my coworkers. There were times I would even hear them snickering and laughing behind my back, especially the Soldiers who I still outranked. I guess in their minds they too were wondering why I wasn't being promoted.

I was allowed to come in late, work through my lunch each day so I could leave early. Some days my son would even come to work with me. He would sit in the car for hours until I got off. Sometimes he would come inside and sit at my desk and sleep. Imagine that, having my adult son come to work with me. I am sure we were the topic of several small group discussions. But, I never complained. I kept thanking God for allowing me to have leaders who were compassionate and understanding to my needs of having to be my son's caregiver. But since I am confessing…I *was* hurt and deeply ashamed.

Gosh, this caregiving life really takes a toll on me. My son is a severe traumatic brain injury survivor. He sustained his injury when he only 11 years old. He's 31 now! This was a big shock to me because it was suddenly and unexpected and I didn't understand very many things about brain injury. Heck, to be honest…I didn't know *anything* about brain injury. I am so grateful God spared his life and allowed him to have a second chance at life. But, I gotta be honest, not in my wildest dream did I ever think life would be this way.

Caregiving is tough and exhausting. Watching someone physically and emotionally decline comes with tons of challenges. As his caregiver, I want to monitor his mood and protect his health and safety so he can experience a good quality of life. But, sometimes I ask myself, "How much longer can I continue caregiving? It seems like there is no end in sight." As my son's caregiver, I don't want to make him feel like he is a burden. Although he completely has no insight of how much I sacrifice because I try so hard to be pleasant and provide for him with a smile, I often feel like I can't go on.

Here comes another confession: "I have no life of my own, and sometimes I am really truly sick of it!" I often feel like Cinderella, at the bidding of those around me, and only able to dream of the life that I want. Sometimes I feel so trapped, like I am not living my own life. Like I somehow got stuck in a role and expectations that I don't want to deal with on a daily basis!

Burnout was something I had experienced within months of initially being his caregiver. I constantly found myself in a state of emotional, mental, and physical exhaustion. I simply lacked the physical and emotional support I needed. Well, heck, since I am confessing...most times I *still* do! Managing the stress levels in my life is not a priority. Yes, I know it should be. Yes, I know I am not only hurting myself but my son as well. But, dang it, I simply don't have the support I need! I can't even remember how many times I've had to cancel or reschedule personal appointments due to my caregiving responsibilities. Feeling powerless is my number one contributor to the burnout I experience. Feeling incapable of just making things all better for us all has caused me to experience some of the darkest days of my life.

Sometimes I just cry and tell myself this must be a punishment of some kind. After all, I didn't always listen to my parents growing up. The Bible clearly told me to honor my mother and father....well, since I *am confessing*...I didn't always do that! I talked back, was disobedient at times, and even lied to them on several occasions. And, being a young mother, I made some pretty stupid decisions that really affected not only me, but also my children. I didn't always put their needs first, which now I look back on and hate myself for. I didn't always trust God with all my heart, mind, and soul. So yea, that's it. "I am reaping what I had sown," is what I often thought!

Depression tried to overtake me several times, but by the grace of God it never prevailed. When you're waiting for something outside you to make your world different, then you're not in charge of yourself. You're allowing someone else to be in control of you, your life, and how you feel. I had to do something, and it needed to be drastic! If I didn't, this caregiving life was going to eventually take me out. Then what would happen to my son? Who would be there for him? Who would he be able to count on? Who would have the patience to listen to him talk about the same subject over and over and over during the day? Who would answer the same questions he would ask at least ten times a day without getting frustrated or aggravated?

When I begin to think about these things, it dawned on me I needed to get myself together. I was brought up in the church, so I knew and understood the power of prayer. Heck, when we first had our accident I prayed like I had never prayed before. I cried out to God for wisdom and understanding about what was going on. I asked Him to heal my son and no matter what it looked like with my physical eyes to never let me stop seeing beyond that. So, I knew and understood what I needed to do in order to get a grip on the overwhelming thoughts and challenges that had begun to consume me.

One day, as I looked at myself in the mirror, I realized I was not the person I used to be. I hated what I saw. My hair was thinning and uncombed, I was overweight, my skin looked discolored and blotchy, and my eyes looked puffy and red. I realized I was on a rollercoaster ride with many highs, lows, twists and turns. You know how frustrating it is when you know you are capable of accomplishing so much more but you can't because you have allowed life and the challenges you are facing pull you to an all-time low. At that moment I knew I had to make a decision. *Do I give up and stop looking in the mirror or do I become determined to find that person I once loved when I would look in the mirror before I became a caregiver?*

For me, I refused to give up. I wasn't happy, and I didn't want to spend the rest of my life feeling like this. I didn't want to give up on life, even though there were times when life didn't seem worth living. Oh yea, by that way, that's *another* confession! Yes, there were times when I thought to myself, "This is just too much to bear, Lord, just let it end." Sometimes for me…and even sometimes for my son. I would think to myself that his life would be so much better if he was in Heaven with Jesus. Shame on me!!!! I would literally hate myself when that thought would even enter my mind. I would literally cry out to God for Him to *please* help me stop thinking that way. I pleaded with God to keep my mind stayed on Him and for Him to keep me in perfect peace. I knew the enemy wanted to take us out.

You see, I knew deep in my heart God was doing something behind the scenes through my son and I; I just didn't know what. I wasn't able to look through my spiritual eyes because the hurt was so deep; it was crippling me in areas of my spiritual life. I knew my son needed me to be here as well as the rest of my family. I knew I wanted to see my grandchildren grow up and enjoy spending summers with their Nana, Papa, and Uncle Mylon. Even if we weren't always able to visit all the places we wanted to, we enjoyed ourselves thoroughly at the places we did go. I knew I had to make some changes….and, I knew I had to make them fast.

So, this is what I did to save myself. I wanted a happy life. I deserved it as a caregiver, and so do you. So, here is the good news, the bad news, and some great news. We all know the story of Cinderella and how she had a fairy godmother that answered her prayer and granted her wish to attend the king's ball. Well, I realized I could be my very own fairy godmother! Yeeeessss!!! That's the good news. I could speak life into the lifeless situations in my life that were weighing me down. I could call those things that were not into existence in my life as though they were! I could use my words to create the change I needed to see in my life. Would it be easy? Probably not and would surely take some effort. Effort…? Yes, effort, so for some, that may feel like bad news.

But don't fret at the thought of having to put forth the effort…because now, here is the *great* news! You don't have to pretend to call upon someone with a magic wand, and big beautiful white gown and all that. All you have to do is go to God in prayer! Yes, that's it! That's the great news, and the best news of all!

What would you wish for? What would you wish to go away? What would you wish to create? What challenges of caregiving would you want diminished? What things would you want your loved one to be able to do they may not be capable of doing? What things would you want in place that would make your life as a caregiver more manageable?

Write those down, please. It's important to write them down so you can physically see when God works them out and you are able to cross it off the list. This is a very important step! Now, pick one of those things you wrote down. Pick the one that you're the most drawn to. The one that jumps off the page or you feel a shift in your belly when you read it.

Now, close your eyes and say this prayer:

"Dear God,

I know you are all knowing and all doing. You remind me in your Word that I can bring my burdens to You and leave them there. As I come to You right now, I feel like I'm carrying a thousand brick loads of weariness and worries. My shoulders are not wide enough, my heart is not big enough, and my wisdom is not deep enough to fix this. So right now at this moment, oh merciful and mighty Jesus, as I come before You, I unload these needs at Your feet. Only You know why there's such an abundance of brokenness, confessions, guilt, and sadness assembling on my doorstep at this time. So, where else can I go but to You?

When darkness tiptoes in, give me light; when hopelessness stifles my soul and mutes me, give me hope; when doubts attacks me, give me faith; when nothing seems sure, give me trust; when ideas disappear, give me vision; when I start to lose my way, be my guide! Help me not be afraid of the emotional chaos, turmoil, and confusion that certain burdens bring. Help me know how to rely on your presence more than I rely on my words. I want to be aware of my limits, but I want to be even more aware of your never-ending mercy, grace, power, and peace. Help me fulfill the role you have given me as a caregiver as I look to you daily for strength, wisdom, and grace. You've said You give Your greatest battles to Your strongest Soldiers. So, thank You for choosing me and for finding me worthy of this call. In the mighty name of Jesus, Amen!"

Immediately after the prayer, sit quietly and allow God to speak to you. Listen as He shares with you what needs to happen in order to move towards the magic that this change will create. Listen as He shares with you the necessary next step to take. If He doesn't answer immediately, don't get discouraged and give up, simply repeat the prayer as many times as needed and each time…wait, and listen for Him to respond.

Keep in mind the response could come in very subtle ways. Learning the voice of God is a process and can be learned. Generally, God speaks to us in four ways. The reason I say generally is because God is so creative! He can find a million ways to make His will audible and visible to us. Hence, for the most part, He normally speaks to us through: His word, His people, His still small voice, or circumstances.

I know you are asking yourself how this happens. Let's say you go to God in prayer. You spend time with Him, ask Him what you want, and seek His will. As you are doing this, you get this feeling in the pit of your tummy of what you should do, but you just aren't really sure, so you wait and continue to seek Him. Somewhere along your path of waiting and seeking, He speaks through His word *or* someone else *or* some situation and you realize it was what you were feeling all along! Suddenly, you recognize, "Oh, that was God speaking to me!" As you continue to seek Him, you will learn His voice. It will become more and more noticeable, and before long you will recognize His voice. You will be able to identify that it's indeed His voice on the other end of the phone and become more comfortable acting upon that still small voice.

So see, really, this is about you and the power you possess inside. It's about the magic you can create in your own life while you are traveling this caregiver journey. You're in charge. Your words have power. You have the power to choose. So look in the mirror, pick up your wand (Bible), and use it wisely.

Mirror mirror on the wall…..

"God is within her *(me)*, she *(I)* will not fall."

– Psalms 46:5

HOW DOES THIS CONNECT WITH YOU AS A CAREGIVER?

NOW...WHAT IS YOUR CONFESSION AS A CAREGIVER AS IT RELATES TO THIS TOPIC?

"Give your circumstance over to Jesus and be confident that He's got it all under control. Your life will change dramatically once you unleash your faith."

— Joyce Meyer

"CAREGIVER'S AFFIRMATION"

I AM grateful for my life just the way it is.

I AM grateful for my family and love them just the way they are.

Today, I will create my own sunshine.

I AM whole and powerful, perfect, and strong.

I AM open to learning lessons of growth daily.

I AM not perfect and will not try to be.

I WILL speak life into the person I care for daily.

I WILL stay positive, even when I don't feel like it.

I WILL accept the person I care for just as they are.

I WILL think positive each and every day.

I WILL smile, even on the bad days.

I WILL do the best I can.

I WILL not try to be all things to all people at any given time.

I WILL not be afraid to say NO when I need to.

I WILL not feel guilty to take care of myself.

I WILL be my own best friend and encourage myself daily.

I WILL be the best caregiver I can be.

I CAN, and I WILL because

I AM A CAREGIVER!

NOTE TO SELF

(Begin with "I am...")

SCRIPTURES THAT SPEAK LIFE AND GIVE YOU STRENGTH

Philippians 4:6,7 (NLT) "Don't worry about anything; instead, pray about everything. Tell God what you need, and thank him for all he has done."

Matthew 11: 28-30 (NLT) "Then Jesus said, 'Come to me, all of you who are weary and carry heavy burdens, and I will give you rest. Take my yoke upon you. Let me teach you, because I am humble and gentle at heart, and you will find rest for your souls. For my yoke is easy to bear, and the burden I give you is light."

Proverbs 3:5-6 (GNT) "Trust in the Lord with all your heart. Never rely on what you think you know. Remember the Lord in everything you do, and he will show you the right way."

Psalms 118:24 (GNT) "This is the day of the Lord's victory; let us be happy, let us celebrate!"

Psalms 121:1-2 (GNT) "I look to the mountains; where will my help come from? My help will come from the Lord, who made heaven and earth.."

2 Corinthians 12:9 (GNT) "But his answer was: "My grace is all you need, for my power is greatest when you are weak." I am most happy, then, to be proud of my weaknesses, in order to feel the protection of Christ's power over me.

Galatians: 5:22-23 (GNT) "But the Spirit produces love, joy, peace, patience, kindness, goodness, faithfulness, humility, and self-control. There is no law against such things as these."

Ephesians 2:9-10 (NIV) "...not by works, so that no one can boast. For we are God's handiwork, created in Christ Jesus to do good works, which God prepared in advance for us to do."

Isaiah 41:10 (NIV) "Do not fear, for I am with you; do not be dismayed, for I am your God. I will strengthen you, I will help you, yes, I will uphold you with My righteous right hand."

Isaiah 40:3 (NIV) "...but those who hope in the Lord will renew their strength. They will soar on wings like eagles; they will run and not grow weary, they will walk and not be faint."

Matthew 6:34 (NIV) "Therefore do not worry about tomorrow, for tomorrow will worry about itself. Each day has enough trouble of its own."

Lamentations 3:32-33 (GNT) "He may bring us sorrow, but his love for us is sure and strong. He takes no pleasure in causing us grief or pain."

Luke 24:36 (NIV) "While they were still talking about this, Jesus himself stood among them and said to them, "Peace be with you."

Philippians 4:19 (NIV) "And my God will meet all your needs according to the riches of his glory in Christ Jesus".

Psalm 46:1 (NIV) "God is our refuge and strength, an ever-present help in trouble."

Isaiah 40:29 (NIV) "He gives strength to the weary and increases the power of the weak."

Colossians 3:1-2 (NIV) "Since, then, you have been raised with Christ, set your hearts on things above, where Christ is, seated at the right hand of God. Set your minds on things above, not on earthly things."

Proverbs 4:23 (NIV) "Above all else, guard your heart, for everything you do flows from it."

Jeremiah 29: 11 (NIV) *"For I know the plans I have for you", declares the Lord, "plans to prosper you and not harm you, plans to give you hope and a future."*

2 Timothy 1:7 (NLT) *"For God has not given us a spirit of fear and timidity, but of power, love, and self-discipline."*

Numbers 6:24-26 (GNT) *"May the Lord bless you and take care of you; May the Lord be kind and gracious to you; May the Lord look on you with favor and give you peace*

ABOUT THE AUTHORS

Twylia G. Reid obtained a B.S. Degree in Business Administration at Trident University International, and is a 20-year US Army disabled retiree. She is a Best-Selling, Multi-Award-Winning, multi-published non-fiction Author, 2019 Trinity Nonprofit Awards Finalist, 2019 Blacks In Government Featured Speaker, 2019 110th NAACP Conference Featured Author/Panelist Moderator, 2019 Unspoken Wounds Women Veteran's Portrait of Personal Courage Award Recipient, 2019 ACHI (Strength In Sisterhood) Magazine Woman of Achievement & Author of the Year Award Nominee, 2018 48th Congressional Legislative Caucus Featured Author, 2019 Winner of The Authors Show Health/Fitness/Wellness Top Female Author, 2018 Winner of The Authors Show Female Non-Fiction Author, 2017 American Book Fest Best Book Awards Finalist, The Huffington Post Expert Feature Series "Who's Who –10 Black Female Experts to Watch in 2018" selected, and the 2017 Indie Author Legacy Award Author of the Year finalist.

She is a native of Mississippi who currently resides in Savannah, GA. A self-published author and coach, her ability to take her life's challenges and turn them into books to empower, educate, and enlighten others has allowed her to write content for survivors of traumatic events and their caregivers by teaching them how to create the life they desire in spite of the challenges faced after their tragedy. She is a woman who truly loves God and loves God's people. She's very passionate about her Christian walk and call into ministry, and grateful for the gift God has entrusted her with and uses it for the advancement of His Kingdom.

She's the Founder and CEO of **Broken Wings, Inc.**, a 501(c)3 Nonprofit Organization that provides resources and prevention insight to traumatic brain injury survivors and their families, and the founder of **Broken Wings Brain Injury Empowerment Group**, an online brain injury support group. She's the Founder and CEO of **When Heaven Speaks, LLC – Book Coaching & Publishing**, minister, speaker, brain injury community advocate, and the Executive Producer/Host of the **Conquerors Café** on Blog Talk Radio, which spotlight authors, entrepreneurs, and survivors who've endured horrific life-changing hardships ready to share their testimonies of hope and healing with the world.

To date, Twylia has authored 16 titles, with the following being #1 Best Sellers: "**Broken Wings**" written to help others understand the life of a brain injury survivor and his caregiver's journey through his recovery; "**What Do You Do…When Caregivers Need Care Given,**" a resource for those operating in the role as a caregiver to those with chronic or lifelong illnesses; "**From Tragedy To Working Strategies,**" a resource guide that teaches survivors strategies to help them turn their traumatic events into empowering moments; and "**Just Because I Have A Brain Injury Doesn't Mean…**" coauthored with her traumatic brain injured son highlighting things brain injury survivors want you to know and understand.

Grateful for the support she's received, and passionate about her role as a traumatic brain injury advocate and caregiver, as the visionary author of this anthology, inspiring and motivating others is what she lives for. Empowering, educating, and enlightening others is her calling. Her mantra is "Aspiring to Inspire Others"!

Books she's written: "Affirmations for the Mind, Body, and Soul" A Guide For Survivors of Traumatic Events, "SOARING By the Power of God" 31-Day Devotional For Spirit Filled Living, "When Caregivers Need Care Given Daily Journal", "My Journey Goal Setting Journal", "The WORD, the Truth & the Light: Bible Study Notebook", "A Survivor's Goal Planning Journal: A Brain Injury Survivor's Guide to Goal Setting", "Pray Believe Receive Prayer Journal", "BUT FIRST...COFFEE" 6-Month Daily Planner, and "GET IT DONE" To-Do List Planner.

Jill Armijo lives in Lehi, Utah, with her husband, Joe, and their two pooches. Their three boys are grown and so far they have one granddaughter, the cutest human alive. Since she was sixteen, Jill has volunteered in her church in various capacities, mostly with children. She helped her parents care for three grandparents growing up, and she had cared for Joe, a veteran with Gulf War Illness, since 1997. She has been a physical therapist assistant, which she loves, for almost thirty years, and is also a health coach who helps caregivers thrive and find happiness as they create the life they want while serving in a challenging circumstance. Jill also enjoys nature, fitness and nutrition, travel, reading, and writing. She mostly enjoys spending time with her family, regardless of what they're doing.

Contact Information:
Website: www.jillarmigo.com
Email: jilldawnarmijo@gmail.com
Facebook: TLC for Caregivers
Instagram: @jarmiji1962

Tamara Newborn is a native of Rock Island, Illinois, but now lives north of Dallas, Texas, with her husband, daughter, and son. She obtained a bachelors in political science from Philander Smith College in Little Rock, Arkansas and a master's degree in criminal justice. Her bachelors and master's degrees fueled her passion to write both fiction and non-fiction novels. She is the author of **"Making it Through the Storm."** In her spare time, she enjoys spending time with her family, reading, and writing. As a breast cancer survivor, she spends time spreading awareness and motivating others to make it through their storms.

Contact Information:
Email: Tamaranewborn@gmail.com
Facebook and Twitter: @tamarabnewborn
Instagram: @iamtamarabnewborn

Arvinese I. Reid holds an associate degree in Liberal Arts and a paralegal certificate. She is currently pursuing her BA in Human Services. She is a minister at The Tabernacle of Prayer Revival Center in Dobbs Ferry, New York. She is a residence manger for a nonprofit organization, where she cares and advocates for young adults with developmental disabilities and their families, as well as oversees the staff in the residence.

Arvinese is passionate about her mission and ministry to be used by God as a vessel to reveal the compassion, healing and restorative power of Jesus Christ to everyone, regardless of what they have encountered in life. She is the mother of one daughter, Aaliyah Slaughter, and twin grandchildren, Tori and Terrence Newland.

Contact Information:
Email: arvinese@gmail.com
Facebook: Arvinese Reid

Teraleen Campbell resides in the Washington, DC suburban area where she is a member of Greater Mt. Calvary Holy Church.

She serves with the Ministerial Alliance and the Music Ministry. Teraleen is a certified Coach. One who knows the worth of prayer, she loves to intercede on behalf of the needs of God's people and serves as lead intercessor each month for the Sisters Prayer Call, which is sponsored by Sisters 4 Sisters, Inc.

She became a member of Zeta Phi Beta Sorority, Inc. at the University of Maryland, where she conducted her undergraduate studies. Her ministry extends to Zeta, as she authored the sorority's *"Centennial Prayer"*, facilitates the *Global Day of Prayer* and is a co-author of the *"Faith of Our Founders Devotional"* Book.

Her community involvement includes the Prince George's County March for Babies Committee and Southern Management Corporation, The March of Dimes, and the American Red Cross have recognized her for her involvement and service to the community. She was named one of the DC Metropolitan area's 100 Phenomenal Women in 2015.

Teraleen also co-authored *"Behind the Scenes of a Phenomenal Woman"*, which was released in 2018. She released her first solo book, *"From Carefree to Caregiver"* in the Fall of 2018.

Contact Information:
Website: www.TeraleenCampbell.com
Email: info@teraleencampbell.com
Facebook and Twitter: Teraleen Campbell
Instagram: Teraleen R. Campbell

Barbara A. Williams was born to the late Rev. Ovis and Anne Flournoy in Newark, New Jersey. She attended schools in the Newark and East Orange school districts. Barbara graduated from Northeastern Bible College in Essex Fells, New Jersey, earning a BA in Biblical Studies and Elementary Education. She went on to earn a Masters of Arts in Elementary Education with an emphasis in Critical Thinking.

A strong believer in helping children and giving back to the community, Barbara spent her first year as an educator as a Pre-School teacher at Newark Day Center. In January 2018, after 32 years, Barbara retired from Newark Public Schools as a middle school teacher, which she loved impacting the lives of her students and their families.

A true prayer warrior, and one who understands the power of prayer, her passion to help others is unwavering. Barbara has been married since July 1989 to her husband Noble Williams. She has two daughters, Kyla and Tiffany, and three beautiful grandchildren.

Contact Information:
Email: nobarwil@yahoo.com
Facebook: Barbara Flournoy-Williams

WE WANT TO HEAR FROM YOU

If this book has made a difference in your life,
I would be delighted to hear about it!

Leave a review on Amazon.com

BOOK TWYLIA TO SPEAK AT YOUR NEXT EVENT

Send an email to: info@twyliareid.com

Learn more about Twylia and her journey of hope and healing at:
www.TwyliaReid.com

If you would like to donate to help spread awareness about traumatic brain injury and the devastation it causes families, please visit:

www.brokenwingsinc.org

RECOMMENDED READINGS

Reid, Twylia G. ***When Caregivers Need Care Given.*** Savannah, Georgia: Broken Wings, 2018.

Reid, Twylia G. ***When Caregivers Need Care Given Journal.*** Savannah, Georgia: When Heaven Speaks, LLC, 2019.

FOLLOW TWYLIA ON SOCIAL MEDIA

Facebook Pages:

www.facebook.com/authortwyliareid
www.facebook.com/BWINC
www.facebook.com/conquerorscafe
LinkedIn: www.linkedin.com/in/twyliareid
Twitter: @tgreid02
Instagram: @twyliareid02

WHEN HEAVEN SPEAKS, LLC